Baby Boomer Entrepreneur:
Implementing the Boomer Business Success System ®

The Complete and Proven Guide to Starting a Successful Business, having Financial Freedom with the Lifestyle that You Want while Making a Difference in the World!

Oreste J. D'Aversa

1

PUBLISHER'S NOTE

Copyright © Oreste J. D'Aversa, 2016 All rights reserved.

FIRST EDITION.

ISBN: 978-0-9826283-1-7

Library of Congress Control Number: 2016957448

Published by *Cutting Edge Technology Publishing*.

Dedication...

- This book is dedicated to you the Baby Boomer.

- The generation that has had its ups and downs.

- The generation that keeps getting up when we're down no matter what happens.

- The generation that takes a "lickin' and keeps on tickin'"

- The generation that does the right thing for their kids and parents.

- The generation that knows that success is not just money, it's about family, friends, love and happiness.

- The generation does not give up!

- The generation that knows that dreams do come true ☺

This Page Intentionally Left Blank

About the Author...

Oreste "Rusty" D'Aversa is an Author, Public Speaker, Seminar Leader, Corporate Trainer, Business Coach, Business Consultant and University Lecturer. He has appeared on radio and television helping people with his expertise to be financially prosperous and find their true life's purpose.

He is also an All-Faiths Minister ordained by The New Seminary in New York City, New York (www.GodLovesYouAndMe.org), a Spiritual Coach, Teacher, and Counselor.

His extensive background in the corporate world in the areas of human resources, supervision, training, consulting, marketing and sales, as well as being an entrepreneur working with self-employed entrepreneurs, businesses and corporations, has been a formidable training ground to help those seeking financial prosperity and life purpose with practical methods and proven tools to reach their goals.

He has created the following publications and audio programs:

- SELL More Technology NOW! (Book, Manual with Audio CDs)
- The Small Business Sales Success Guide (Manual with Audio CDs)
- The Step-By-Step Networking Kit (Manual with Audio CDs)
- The Resume Writing Kit (Manual with Audio CDs)
- The Seven Simple Principles of Prosperity (Book, Manual with Audio CDs)
- Discovering Your Life Purpose: The Journey Within (Book, eBook)
- Empowering Your Children in the New Millennium (Book)
- The Lightworker's Guide to Getting Clients (Manual with Audio CDs)
- The 60 Minute Mind-Body-Spirit Workout (Audio CD)
- Killing Writer's Block Dead (Audio CD)
- The Exam Stress Buster (Audio CD)
- Your Healing Temple: Using The Power of Your Mind to Help Heal Your Body (Audio CD)

To learn more about all the products, programs and services he offers go to:

www.OresteDAversa.com

www.MetroSmallBusinessConsultant.com

eMail: OresteDAversa@outlook.com

This Page Intentionally Left Blank

My Story...

I'm a product of an immigrant Italian family. My father was a bricklayer and my mother a stay at home housewife. I started working at 13 years of age delivering papers, being a short order cook at the area marina, a laborer in the construction field, factory work and other odd jobs.

Worked my way through college, graduated with a Bachelor of Science Degree in Political Science in Criminal Justice only to find out most of the jobs were going to returning Vietnam veterans, those with perfect scores on civil service tests or with political contacts (none of which I had). I was accepted for graduate work at American University only to turn it down, thinking I'll be in the same situation two years later with graduate work debt on my hands as well.

I looked at the business market place back then and everyone was saying "computers", so while working a going nowhere job, I went to a technical school and graduated with a 9-month certificate in computer programming and spent the next 20 years in the computer industry. Ten years with one company, doing pre-sales support, training, consulting and technical support. Traveling all over the country about 50% of the time. It was easy and a lot of fun back then, the technology industry was new and fresh. Those of us in the industry were viewed as "the chosen ones" since we knew about technology and how to apply it in the business world as most people just marveled at the technology of those times.

I was downsized after ten years and took a severance package. Ran my own business for a year, didn't know what I was doing. Was good at what I did, but did not understand the workings of running a business, marketing, sales, administration, multiple revenue streams, etc. Made some money but not enough to sustain myself.

Went back to the technology industry, this time in sales. Had ten jobs in ten years! The good thing was every time I changed jobs I was getting raises, the bad thing, it's no way to build stability in your life. The technology companies I worked for are all gone now. They either merged with other companies, or were acquired, ran out of money, went bankrupt, had bad management and went out of business or were lying to the marketplace and were caught.

My last corporate job I really had enough of all the corporate nonsense, politics and being at the mercy of the business marketplace for employment. Then 9/11 hit. I happened to be in "Tower Two" only 2 weeks before the attack doing a sales presentation for the software company I was working for at the time. I still carry the building ID card I was issued to me to this day.

I decided to go back into business for myself. I thought that I was off to a good start, and was going to be an executive recruiter for the software industry, being that I came from there and had a background in the industry. Landed a part time job in an outplacement firm (they deliver job search skills and resume workshops for employers that lay people off) and was doing workshops for those employees that were terminated.

8

They promised me a 3-day work week, which was good as I could build my recruiting business on my days off. Three days a week turned into THREE DAYS A MONTH!!! I knew something was wrong as I could not get a written offer letter from the outplacement firm before I started. Life lessoned learned! When it comes to business always gets it in writing! Unfortunately, that venture failed as I needed the part time job to keep me afloat until I built my business.

After that I did some sales training in my business, as I was a salesperson for over ten years. Met a lot of people that were good at what they did but did not know how to sell their products and services to the market place to get customers. Also during this time, I delivered business consulting, being that I ran my own business, I was and am able to help people with Strategic Planning, Marketing, Sales, Product and Services Packaging and Customer Service. Also, during this time I became an Ordained Minister and continue to be an All Faiths Minister and perform wedding ceremonies and spiritual counseling when my schedule permits.

Then my parents become sick. First my father, then my mother. I am an only child and primary caregiver to my immigrant parents. I have helped them with all of their legal, medical, various government agencies and emotional needs and events that go along with death and dying. Part of being a baby boomer is taking care of your family. I lost everything financially but did what I had to do as a son and as a man. Working when I could, but taking care of my family first.

Now you know my story now. I'm basically a one-person industry. Write my own books, market, sell and deliver my services. Outsource the things I'm not good at or are too time consuming and not profitable for me to do myself. I have either taught myself how to do things, read and continue to read books, take workshops and work with coaches to continue to hone my skills and learn new skills as well. I have done it and continue to do it, and you can do it too! Yes, it does take work, time and financial investment, but the paybacks are immeasurable. You are in charge of your own life! I can "teach you how" to fish and once you "learn how to fish" you will never be hungry again! You will know how and where to create opportunities to create revenue. We're Baby Boomers, we get it done and have fun doing it ☺

Currently, I help baby boomers reach their goals with my **Boomer Business Success System®** (and yes, I own the Trademark on the name ☺ I did it all myself and you can do it too!) starting and running successful businesses, making a difference in the world doing their true "work", and having the financial freedom and lifestyle that we all want. I get to use all of my skills; as a public speaker, business coach, consultant and trainer to help baby boomers on their journey and I'm having a blast doing it!

Table of Contents

Page

This Page Intentionally Left Blank

Chapter 1:   Introduction

Welcome to one of the most exciting, if not **the** most exciting adventure of your life, running your own business. The concepts you will be learning apply to all businesses, big and small alike, whether you want to run a table at a flea market or want to grow a large corporation. Successful businesses, those that last and are profitable, perform all the tasks mentioned here in one form or another. In larger businesses it is done with more people, in smaller businesses it is done with less people and in really small businesses (sole proprietor) it is done by one person. While starting any business is risky at best, performing the tasks mentioned in this book will take things from "a gamble" to more of "a calculated risk" and give you the ability to make less mistakes, and when mistakes are made are able to bounce back quicker with less down time and/or less cost. As we all know, time is money and both time and money need to be invested wisely.

Running your own business can be one of the most rewarding experiences of your life, the freedom to do whatever you want and whenever you want to do it. It can also be one of the worst experiences of your life, consuming every aspect of your life and all your finances. **Being an entrepreneur is not for everyone and not for people that are not willing to do whatever it takes. Doing things, they never have done before or are performing uncomfortable tasks that need to be done in order to run a successful business.** It can also be the most rewarding aspect of your life, taking a concept from thought to creation and delivering your products and/or services. Having a positive impact on other people lives and making money doing so will make you feel like you have made a real difference in this world.

In starting any new business venture, it is always a good practice to contact an attorney and accountant. You want to discuss with your attorney issues such as business liability and how to get proper legal counsel for your business. With your accountant you want to discuss; how you should set up your business from a tax point of view (sole proprietor, LLC, Corporation, etc.), record keeping and other business tax issues you need to know about. Both your attorney and your accountant are members of your business team and are considered to be your "Trusted Advisors". **A trusted advisor, as the term implies, is someone you go to, that you trust, in that particular area of expertise before you make any major business decisions.** Other trusted advisors could be a computer technical person, business consultant/business coach and web site designer.

For baby boomers the challenges are many, besides the issues that all business owners face, there is life as a baby boomer, what that means and all that goes with it. The lack of job security of years ago, dare I say the word "pension", taking care of the children, taking care of the parents, hence being "The Sandwich Generation", maybe even taking care of the grandchildren, the cost of living constantly going up and on and on. There is hope and there are tools that will help you, that will be discussed later on in this book.

To give you a step by step blueprint on how to reach your financial and personal goals I have created the **Boomer Business Success System** ® to give you the tools you need to get started on your journey. These tools consist of personal development techniques, as well as proven business methods used by successful businesses of all sizes.

To help you find your true reason for being here, there is also a section on Personal Fulfillment. Here are some tools to help you find **Your Life's Purpose.** Practical methods and techniques to find your "real self" and what you are here to do, your "work" and not just your job.

On the subject of business, there are five major areas that you need to understand in running a business as illustrated below:

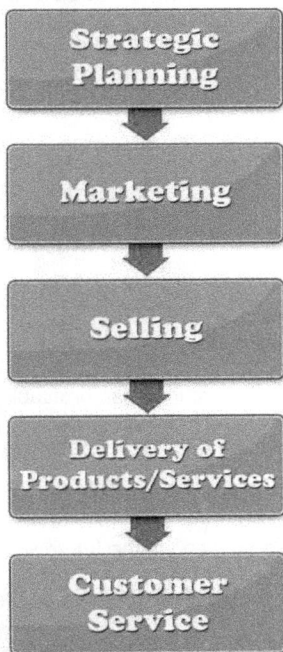

```
┌─────────────────────┐
│ Strategic           │
│ Planning            │
└─────────────────────┘
          ▼
┌─────────────────────┐
│ Marketing           │
└─────────────────────┘
          ▼
┌─────────────────────┐
│ Selling             │
└─────────────────────┘
          ▼
┌─────────────────────┐
│ Delivery of         │
│ Products/Services   │
└─────────────────────┘
          ▼
┌─────────────────────┐
│ Customer            │
│ Service             │
└─────────────────────┘
```

They are **Strategic Business Planning, Marketing, Selling, Delivery of Products and/or Services** and **Customer Service.** Each piece builds upon the one below it. The more you build your business on this model the greater the likelihood that there will be a financial success. Conversely, the more you shortcut this model the less likely you are to succeed. As with everything in life there are exceptions and there are those people who have used nothing and were still successful, but they are the very few and not the rule.

Strategic Business Planning is an organized process of defining the direction, and making decisions on allocating the resources (financial and otherwise) to pursue this direction. Here is where the "tough" questions about your business are discussed, explored and answered. Strategic Planning is viewed as a process for determining where an organization is going over the next year or more.

Marketing is the process of communicating the value of your product(s) and/or service(s) to prospective customers, for the purpose of selling the product(s) and/or service(s). It is a critical business function for attracting customers.

Selling is a series of steps or a process where a buyer exchanges cash for a seller's goods and/or services.

Delivery of Products and/or Services is having standardized methods to deliver your products and/or services to increase profitability.

Customer Service is a series of activities designed to increase the level of customer satisfaction. In doing so customers are more likely to purchase more products and services from your business now and in the future.

Many books have been written and continue to be written on the topics above. **The purpose of this book is to help you establish a basic foundation of knowledge in each of these areas. As your business grows, you may require further knowledge and expertise in a given area of your business.**

This book has been designed to give you practical information and exercises that you can use immediately to help you run a profitable business, increase sales revenues and increase business productivity. These are real world tools that will help you create a business that works for you so you can really be a business owner and not just an employee in your own business.

I have also included a chapter on **Small Business Resources.** There is a wealth of knowledge and resources that are low cost or no cost on the internet and federal, state and local governments provide to help you with your business. These resources will save you a lot of time and money, help you become more productive and help reach your goals quicker.

As the saying goes, "Give a person a fish, and you feed them for a day; show a person how to catch fish, and you feed them for a lifetime". You're being taught here how to fish, to provide for yourself, your family and to achieve the lifestyle you desire. So let's batten down the hatches, weigh anchor, and shove off for richest, prosperous and most fun filled cruise of your life!

NOTES

Chapter 2: What Baby Boomers Need to Know

What is a Baby Boomer?

Baby boomers are people born after World War II between 1946 and 1964. Representing nearly 20% of the American public, baby boomers continue to have a significant impact on the economy. More babies were born in 1946 than ever before: 3.4 million, 20 percent more than in 1945. This was the beginning of the so-called "baby boom." In 1947, another 3.8 million babies were born; 3.9 million were born in 1952; and more than 4 million were born every year from 1954 until 1964, when the boom finally tapered off. By then, there were 76.4 million "baby boomers" in the United States. [1]

The Statistical Data

Statistics:

77.3 million Baby Boomers (as of 2008)

1946 - Post World War II

3,411,000 - the number of babies born in the U.S.

9,345.2 per day

389.38 per hour

6.49 per minute

1954 - Post Korean War

4,078,000 - the number of babies born in the U.S.

11,172.6 per day

465.53 per hour

7.76 per minute

1957 - The Year the Boom Peaked

4,300,000 - the number of babies born in the U.S.

11,780.8 per day

490.87 per hour

8.18 per minute

1964 - The End of an Era

4,027,000 - the number of babies born in the U.S.

11,002.7 per day

458.48 per hour

7.64 per minute

January 1, 1996 - The first of the baby boomers turn 50.

January 1, 2011 - The first of the boomers turns 65. Approximately two-thirds of all seniors 65 and over and 60% of those 50-64 have at least one chronic disease.

Boomers make up approximately 25% of the total U.S. population of 311,591,917. (as of July 2011)

Boomers work past retirement, only 11% plan to stop working entirely. A survey by AARP reveals most boomers plan to work "until they drop".

1979 - The year the U.S. divorce rate peaks. There are 2,331,000 marriages and 1,181,000 divorces, according to the U.S. Census, and the first of the boomers turn 33. Thirty years later, 39% of boomers have been divorced and the national divorce rate is declining.

Approximately $8.4 trillion will be inherited by boomers from their grandparents, parents, and others.

December 31, 2029 - The last of the boomers will turn 65. The 65+ population segment is projected to double to 71.5 million by 2030 and grow to 86.7 million by 2050. Possibly eighty million plus will be on Medicare and Social Security. [2]

Economic Data

- The 55+ age group controls more than three-fourths of America's wealth (ICSC).

- 78 million Americans who were 50 or older as of 2001 controlled 67% of the country's wealth, or $28 trillion (U.S. Census and Federal Reserve).

- Boomers and seniors have seen a decrease in their median family net worth, however, they still have a net worth 3x of younger generations (Economic Policy Institute).

- Boomers' median household income is 55% greater than post-Boomers and 61% more than pre-Boomers. They have an average annual disposable income of $24,000 (US Government Consumer Expenditure Survey).

- The 50+ have $2.4 trillion in annual income, which accounts for 42% of all after-tax income (U.S. Consumer Expenditure Survey).

- Adults 50 and older own 65% of the aggregate net worth of all U.S. households (U.S. Consumer Expenditure Survey).[3]

Some Not So Good Economic Data

- 15% expect never to retire.

- Do not feel they have saved enough money, early enough, to be prepared for retirement.

    - On average, start saving for retirement at age 35

    - 27% say they won't have the income they need to live comfortably in retirement (the same goes for 35% of retirees.)

    - Most say lack of saving for retirement is one of the biggest mistakes of their lives.

    - 27% expect to have trouble paying medical bills.
    - 62% are not confident that Medicare will provide consistent benefits throughout retirement.

- Only 1 in 3 adults in their 50s have attempted to create a retirement plan.

- Only 2 in 3 of that 33% have succeeded

- Carrying higher debt: the overall debt for 55+ households more than doubled from 1992 to 2007 [4]

The Boomer Business Success System ®

I created the Boomer Business Success System ® to give baby boomers practical tools to reach their financial and personal lifestyle goals. The baby boomer (being one myself) has challenges on multiple areas in their life and each area requires tools, methods and techniques to deal with every changing challenge. While some topics and subject areas may seem like "new age mumbo jumbo" and others like subjects you would learn in a business school of higher learning, I assure you that once you start using all the exercises in this book you will see how they all fit together and help you with your success, both financially and in your personal life, as well as managing the stress that comes with modern day living.

Tools to Increase Productivity, Reduce Stress and be more creative to get more done in less time and be happy doing it

The following tools, methods and techniques in this chapter are not all directly related to business; however I assure you they will help your business bottom line. Originally I had planned on placing them at them at the end of the book, however I feel they will help you while you start building your business. Much of what you will be learning is not difficult however it does involve a massive amount of decision making, with each decision has a "pro and a con" side to it and impacting your business in time and money.

No matter whom you work with an attorney, accountant, business coach, consultant, etc., this is <u>YOUR</u> business and <u>YOU</u> are ultimately responsible for <u>YOUR</u> decisions. These tools will help you achieve clarity of mind to make the proper decisions for your business at that particular point in time. Some tools and techniques maybe be new to you and others may sound farfetched, but I assure you when you are about to make major business decisions they will be a welcome addition to your "business tool box". There is an old business saying that goes; "if the only tool you have is a hammer, then every problem looks like a nail". You need different tools to solve different problems. As a Swiss Army knife is a good item to carry in your pocket as it can handle any type of emergency, these tools are good to have in your business tool kit to help guide you and help in your decision making process.

A. Personal Behaviors

1 – Change Your Thinking Change Your Life

Be prepared to change the way you think about certain things relative to business. This does not mean compromising your beliefs, but it may mean changing your likes and dislikes. Say you've built a widget (widget is the term used for a thing) in various colors. Now the hot color is this hot lime green, which is the color used in construction and roadwork apparel. You personally don't like it, you actually hate it, but the marketplace has told you it wants your widget made in that color. What do you do? Do you go against your likes or give the market what it wants? You and only you can make that decision. The decision YOU make is YOUR decision, be it right or wrong from a business point of view, only you can decide and deal with the repercussions that go with it. Both positive or negative.

2 – Be Flexible and Adaptable

Being flexible and adaptable is the new mantra of the new millennium. Personal life and work life no longer fit into nice and neat little boxes in the real world. Sometimes a Sunday afternoon will be work and a Tuesday afternoon will be play. Be prepared for doing things right and everything going wrong. As well as doing things wrong, things working right, and every combination thereof. You get the idea. Computers will crash, vendors will be late in delivering supplies for your business and the car does break down on the way to the biggest potential client you have ever met. You will rise to the occasion. You will improvise, overcome, adapt (got this from the United States Marines – it's just a good way to live).

3 – Wear Many Hats

Be prepared to wear many hats, meaning doing different functions and tasks for your business. If you start off as a sole proprietor, you will be the CEO making strategic decisions about your business. You will be the Marketing Manager making decisions how to and where to and who to market your products/services in the market place. You will be a Salesperson closing deals. You will be a Field Person delivering and implementing your products and services. And a host of other functions relative to making your business successful and profitable. In time you can hire people to do some of the tasks. All this may sound daunting and overwhelming at first, and it is, but I assure you once you start closing your first deals and you work out the kinks that every business has, it becomes fun, enjoyable and very profitable.

4 – Listen to Success Not Failure

Many people will be giving you advice on running <u>YOUR</u> business. A word of advice here. **Only listen to people who have <u>SUCCESSFULLY</u> run their own business and have done or are doing what you do or something similar to it.** Many people are quick to give advice on other people's situations only to find out they have either never done it on their own or were failures doing it. Success breeds success and failure breeds failure. Learn from proven successful people, watch what they are doing, do what they do. Want to be a millionaire, learn from a millionaire. Want to be successful (whatever that means to you) then learn from successful people.

5 – Fear and FUD

When starting any new venture, it is only natural that you may have some fear and/or FUD (Fear, Uncertainty and Doubt). It's important to manage and overcome these things as if they are not handled properly, they can hold you back from your success. The best way to handle them is to plan and prepare as much of your business as possible. I asked one of my clients about this as he appeared to be fearless and lucky much of the time with his business offerings and tasks. He told me, "Luck is when preparation meets opportunity" - Seneca. Though he may not have been the first to coin the phrase it certainly has much merit. That's why many successful businesses spend time in planning so they can be prepared as much as possible for the unforeseen events in the marketplace. There are some exercises later in this chapter that will be helpful as well.

6 – Discipline

To be successful in any field of endeavor you must have discipline. This is your business, not someone else's business. If a business task needs to be done by Monday at 9am it is your responsibility that it's done by then or preferably sooner. Being disciplined is one of the major keys to your success.

Many people want to write a book and say they don't have the time to do it. The issue is the discipline to take 30 minutes each day to write that book. This may mean getting up 30 minutes earlier each day to write or stay up 30 minutes later in the evening to write. Whatever you need to do to find those 30 minutes each day to write you must do it!

Disciple is a habit. Like all habits, it takes time to develop. Once you develop the habit of being disciplined you will get so much more accomplished each day and will be "working smart" as well as hard on your business.

7 – Prosperity

What is Prosperity? Webster's dictionary defines prosperity as, "the condition of being successful or thriving; especially: economic well-being". Defining Prosperity really depends with whom you are talking to about this subject. To some people it means money, wealth and financial success. To others, it's health, peace of mind, love, friends and family. **Prosperity means whatever you want it to mean.** There is no right or wrong answer. I am certain there are as many different expressions of prosperity as there are people on the planet.

How do we invoke Prosperity? How do we make it come to us, into our lives? There are various methods for bringing prosperity into our lives. You will learn some practical exercises to achieve a rich, happy and joyous life!

Prosperity Exercise:

1. What does prosperity mean to you?

_____

_____

_____

2. What do you need to be prosperous? – clearly define with specific examples

_____

_____

_____

3. How can you help others to be prosperous?

_____

_____

_____

B. Mind and Physical Exercises

Baby boomers usually have started working with our backs at a young age, but now most of the work is performed by our minds, yet in our society we don't teach people how to relax or work their minds properly. When you are physically tired you rest your body with sleep, maybe a massage, but how do you rest your mind? Especially from the massive amounts of stress that comes with being a baby boomer. One big stressor is being a part of the "sandwich generation" (The Sandwich Generation is a generation of people who care for their aging parents while supporting their own children).

Below are a few exercises that will help you manage stress. Do them often and you will be able to handle whatever comes your way in life. We cannot totally eliminate stress in our lives, but we can manage how we handle it.

<u>DO NOT</u> PERFORM THESE EXERCISES WHILE DRIVING.

ALWAYS BE AWARE OF YOUR SURROUNDINGS WHILE PERFORMING FOCUSED ACTIVITIES.

Exercise - Breathing for Relaxation

Taking deep **s-l-o-w** breaths in and out will help you relax.

The benefit of this exercise is to help one become calm, peaceful and centered.

1. Take a slow, deep **breath in** for a count up to four – one, two, three, four.

2. Then slowly **exhale out** for a count up to four – one, two, three, four.

3. Take a slow, deep **breath in** for a count up to four – one, two, three, four.

4. Then slowly **exhale out** for a count up to four – one, two, three, four.

5. Take a slow, deep **breath in** for a count up to four – one, two, three, four.

6. Then slowly **exhale out** for a count up to four – one, two, three, four.

7. Perform this exercise 3 or 4 times and notice how relaxed you become.

   You can do this exercise as often as you like.

Exercise - Meditation

Meditation is aligning **Mind, Body, Emotions and Spirit**, so that these components function as one. Meditating is the practice of quieting the mind of all its chatter to enable you to be open to the thoughts of the Universe.

The benefit of this exercise is to become centered in one's self.

1. This is the **"1 – 2 – 3 – 4" Method of Meditation**.

2. Take a slow, deep **breath in** for a count up to four – one, two, three, four.

3. Then slowly **exhale out** for a count up to four – one, two, three, four.

4. Take a total of 3 or 4 slow, deep breaths.

5. Then just say to yourself, in your mind, **"1 – 2 – 3 – 4"** over and over again.

6. The purpose of this is to focus your mind on the counting and away from the chatter that is with us in our mind.

7. There is no right way or wrong way to perform this meditation. Do what you feel is comfortable and natural for you. There is no need for stress or strain. In time you will have no need for counting **"1 – 2 – 3 – 4"** you will be able to close your eyes and go into a calm, relaxing and peaceful meditative state.

You can do this exercise in the morning before you start your day for 5 minutes and just before you end your day, for 5 minutes.

Visualization

Visualization refers to the practice of seeking to affect the outer world by changing one's thoughts. You can choose to visualize anything you desire in life, including your life purpose. You may want to record this exercise and play it back to yourself. Use visualization to see in your mind's eye the type of prosperity you are seeking.

Exercise - Visualization for Your Prosperity

The benefit of this exercise is to help you create an environment that can help you visualize prosperity.

1. Find a place that is quiet and you will not be disturbed. Now close your eyes and take a nice deep breath. Take a nice deep, deep breath. Relax your mind; relax your body. You are totally calm and totally relaxed; totally calm and totally relaxed.

2. Count from four down to the number one. With every number you count, I would like you to take a deep breath, and each time say the word "relax," Relax and exhale the breath from your body. With every number you count, take a deep breath, and each time say the word "relax", relax and allow the breath to exhale from your body.

Four, take a nice deep breath (pause) and relax.

Three, take a nice deep breath (pause) and relax.

Two, take a nice deep, deep breath (pause) and relax.

One, deep breath (pause)... and relax. Relax your thoughts; relax your body.

Very good, now continue to breathe normally.

3. Now count from four down to one again. Mentally release each group of muscles that is called to your attention.

Four, release the muscles in the head and face. Just release and relax. Feel your head slowly drop forward if that is comfortable for you.

Three, release the muscles in your neck and shoulders. Just release and relax any stress and any strain.

Two, release the muscles in your back and allow your hands to fall to your sides if you wish.

One, release the muscles in your stomach and feel the relaxation flow down through your legs and feet.

Like a series of dominoes, all the muscles in your body begin at the top of your head and flow into one another as each one releases and relaxes.

With every beat of your heart, with every breath that you take, you will become more relaxed, calmer, more relaxed, calmer...

... Good. Continue to use your imagination. Imagine the warm, golden sun going down into your skin and melting deeply within every cell of your body.

4. The gentle warmth flows over through your muscles, allowing them to relax. Release and relax all of the tension; all of the strain.

Feel the muscles in your neck and shoulders expand.

Notice how you feel - without stress - free in your body and mind. Your heart rate and breathing are calm and relaxed. Your muscles are totally relaxed. Totally calm, totally relaxed. Totally calm, totally relaxed.

5. Now, think about a time in the not too distant **future**. In a vision, see yourself living the life you want to lead. A life full of prosperity, whatever prosperity means to you, and enjoying the lifestyle you want to lead. It could be a life filled with lots of money, good health, loved ones, friends, whatever you want it to mean.

What type working are you doing? Where are you doing it and with what type of people? Use all of your senses. Are there any specific smells? See it. Touch it. Experience it! Just let it come to you...

6. See yourself being prosperous. Being happy, fulfilled, you are full of joy and wonderment. So happy to be prosperous and living the lifestyle you choose!

LONG PAUSE...

7. When I count to four... you will slowly awake...feeling good and alert. Remembering everything you experienced in your visualization and able to write it down if you wish....One...you're beginning to come back...Two... feel the energy start flowing through your body...Three... moving your fingers and toes... more and more awake...feel the energy running through your body ...Four... breathing in wakeful energy... clearing your head... balancing your energies... feeling wonderful in every way..., opening your eyes... fully coming back... fully back... wide awake... and ready to go...

You can do this exercise once a day.
You can do it more if you like.

Brainstorming

Brainstorming is a group or individual creativity technique by which efforts are made to find a conclusion for a specific problem by gathering a list of ideas spontaneously contributed by its member(s). There is also brainstorming software. Google the words "Brainstorming" and "Mind Mapping software" for more information. The software, much of it free, will be a very helpful to guide you visually to what you would like to accomplish with your business. Below is a sample of the product I use called **SimpleMind** (http://www.simpleapps.eu/simplemind/). I use it on my tablet to brainstorm while on the couch.

Example of brainstorming using mind mapping software:

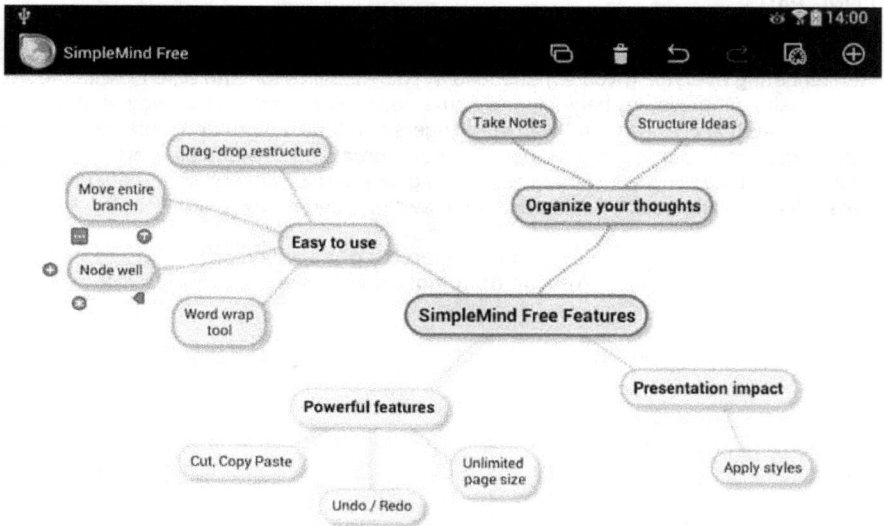

Vision Boards

A Vison Board is a large piece of paperboard to post images to depict goals and dreams in all areas of your life, or in just one specific area that you are focusing on, which inspire you and make you feel good.

An Example Vision Board:

Exercise   -   Physical Exercise

Before doing any new or different types of exercises, check with your physician.

Physical activity will contribute in our growth process. Physical exercise can improve the cardiovascular functions and contributes to a healthy skeletal muscle system. Physical exercise and a well-balanced diet will help to regulate weight, and manage stress.

The benefits of this exercise are many; to release excess energy, staying in shape; relaxing the body and the mind, also assists in calming   the   mind   and   spirit.

Other types of physical exercises.

1. Stretching - Stretching exercises are used to prevent injury and prepare your body for exercising all the body muscles. **Stretching** is a powerful part of any exercise program. **Stretching** works in conjunction with muscles to improve athletic performance, joint flexibility and maintain good body posture. Stretching warms up the muscles.

2. Walking - Walking is not only a great exercise for maintaining health; it's also one of the best exercises to help control weight. There are many benefits to be gained from walking. These can include more energy, deeper and more satisfying sleep, stronger leg muscles, less knee pounding than running, lower body fat, higher metabolic rate and reducing stress. Many students, who walk or exercise, study more effectively and have better recall.

3. Jogging - Jogging is one of the simplest exercise programs, as it produces many benefits. You can do it by yourself. It helps you build a good physique by stimulating your heart rate, relieving stress and toning your muscles. It increases your energy level and it brings a sense of discipline; it is more result oriented than any other type of workout. It also helps burn calories and helps you stay fit.

4. Networking Events with Others – Attending networking events with others, though a simple concept, produces many benefits including and not limited to, meeting new people, interaction and socialization with others and making new contacts that can help you with your life purpose.

5. Yoga - As previously mentioned, Yoga exercises help us to attain body and mental control and achieve a sense of well-being.

6. Martial Arts - The benefits of Martial Arts are many; they teach physical and mental strength training, discipline, leadership skills and how to interact with others. The martial arts have many different styles; offensive and defensive techniques. Both are effective in their benefits to us.

7. Play Team Sports – Regardless of the sport, playing team sports with others in a team environment helps us get along with other people to achieve a common goal. Working together they are all winners.

Exercise - Connecting with Nature

Connecting with nature is an excellent way to feel connected to the planet; to Mother Earth, to feel grounded and calm.

The benefit of this exercise is to understand nature and how important nature and all the plants and animals are in our lives.

1. Grow a Plant - If you cannot go to nature, then bring nature to you by growing a plant. You don't need a lot of space and you can observe nature up close and personal.

2. Hug a Tree – Want to feel nature? Next time you see a tree go give it a nice big hug! Yes, that may seem a little corny, but trees do help us.

3. Go to a Park – Parks are always a good place to go to be with nature. Touch the grass, see the animals, hear the birds, smell the flowers or taste the water (just make sure that the water is clean☺).

4. Go to the Ocean, a Lake, a Stream or Pond – Visit a body of water and observe the fish and wildlife that live there.

5. Go to the Mountains – Connect with nature on a mountain. Take in the fresh, clean, crisp mountain air. Go for a hike with friends or join a club.

6. Go to the Local Animal Shelter – Visit with a friend or with by yourself, a local animal shelter and connect to the animals there. Animals need attention and love too!

7. Go to the Zoo – If you really want to connect with nature, go to a zoo and see all the different animals there. You will learn so much from the different animals from around the world.

C. Business Tools

1 – Use Different Tools for Different Tasks – When You only have a Hammer every Problem Looks like a Nail!

Running your own business is going to require you to have different tools in your "business tool kit" to do different tasks to operate a successful business. If you are a task oriented person, then you are going to need people skills. Conversely, if you are a people oriented people you are going to need the disciple of doing tasks, processes and procedures. While you can outsource some of the things you don't like to do or can't do, remember, the more you outsource the less profit you are going to make. You don't need to be a master at everything but a "jack of all trades" mentality certainly does help when running your own business. Running your own business does require you to have an open mind about learning new things. The more you can do for yourself, the more savings in time and money you will achieve for yourself in the long run. I never thought I would be writing books, let alone having my articles appear in trade magazines, and being on radio and even television. I taught myself how to do this, by reading books on the subjects, observing what others like me did and asking questions. You can do all this as well. It may take a little bit of an investment of time and maybe some money, but you will use these new skills the rest of your life in and out of your business.

2 – Embrace Technology

Technology is here to stay and will be a very important part of your business. You do not need to become a "tech head" but you do need to have a fundamental understanding and working knowledge of technology what it does and how it can expand your business productivity and profitability. Technology has come a long way since I went to technical school learning to punch IBM computer cards to the modern day where mobile phones are basically mobile computers.

If you are not technology savvy start off by going to Google (www.Google.com) and research and download a "Glossary of Computer Terms". This is an excellent starting point to get you familiar with terms and phrases in computing and technology. Next, take class(s) at a local high school and/or college continuing education program. Do as much technology stuff as you can handle and like to do. Outsource the really difficult things, but know enough about what needs to be done so you can have an intelligent conversation with the person doing the work.

3 – Work Smart: Task and Self-Management

Working smart is the name of the game. What does working smart really mean? It means working as intelligently as possible to be productive and make money and lose as little money as possible while doing so. Running a business requires discipline. Discipline in performing tasks, discipline in yourself and discipline in managing time. You will find that your business life will become a series of MBOs (Management By Objectives). Things need to get done and you are the person to do them. So every working day get up and set for yourself a MANAGABLE list of things to get done in your business. I say manageable because manageable helps prime the engine of success. You write twelve business things to do today and only 3 get done. How does that make you feel? How about writing six business things to do today and get them ALL done! Now how does that make you feel? ☺ Slow and steady wins the race in business. Take "calculated risks" and not "gambles" when necessary to move ahead and even catapult your business.

4 – Time and Money, Money and Time the Zen of Managing Both

We've all heard the expression time is money. It has never been as true as when you work for yourself. Every time you make a business decision, and you will be making them daily, you must think about the amount of time it will take and the amount of money you will either be making or losing to do (or participant) in a task. Now keep in mind that you do have to make investments in time and money to further your business, **the challenge is to make more <u>RIGHT</u> decisions that WRONG decisions**. It is an art and science that every business owner hopes to learn and master. The better you get at it the more successful you and your business will be.

5 - Time Management Tools

When running your own business, it's important to develop the disciple of time management. And yes, it is a disciple. In the beginning of any business venture there is much to be done. All of us have the same of hours in the day and days in the week, etc. The trick is to work as productively as possible within these hours. You will find that your business life becomes life by **MBOs** (Management by Objectives). Things need to get done and you have to do them (until you start making enough money to hire a team then you can delegate some things to them).

You need to be mindful of the **"Money Hours"** of your business. The Money Hours are the time of the day in which money is to be made, collected, paid, etc. During these hours, your focus should be on getting money (deals), moving deals along, working with customers and servicing customers. During the Money Hours you are not stuffing envelopes, going to the store, watching television, etc. With that said your money hours may be from 8:00am to 11:30am in the morning and 1:30pm and 4:30pm in the afternoon.

So by using proper time management you can stuff envelopes, go to the store, watch television, etc., before the Money Hours start, at lunchtime and after the Money Hours are over. This time management disciple is a very good habit to get into.

Below are two-time management tools, and are here to get you started. Find the system you like or create your own. All successful people use some sort of time management system to get things done in their world and you should too. Others time management tools can be found at www.MindTools.com mentioned later in this chapter.

I have also included some other business tools in this section that you will need and/or may grow into when the need arises. Do not be intimidated by all these tools and this information. Some you will use immediately, while others will be used at a later date or you will grow into them as your business expands.

The One-Percent Solution*
(Time Management Tool)

- Unless you manage your time you will not be able to manage anything else. The management of your time is the foundation for your effectiveness. (Drucker, 2006, page 11).

- **Four Facts About Time**:

Fact One: Time is a Limited Resource

Fact Two: Time is an Inflexible Resource

Fact Three: There will Always be More Things to do Than Time to do them

Fact Four: Focus, not Efficiency, is the Key to Mastering our Time

- The following is a very simple system that allows you to apply the above principles

- Devote 30 minutes one time each week to access the past week and plan the next week

- Identify **four to six** areas of your life, both personally and professionally, that are your highest priorities.

- Target one or two of the most important steps of action to be accomplished this week for each priority area.

- Schedule your top priority steps of action first in your calendar for the week.

- Devote **five minutes** each day to adjust your schedule and realign with your priorities.

- **Use the A, B, C, D, E Priority Method**

- **A Task:** Top Priority

- **B Task:** Needs to be done this week

- **C Task:** Low Priority to be done by month's end

- **D Task:** Delegate to Someone Else

- **E Task:** Eliminate or do not do the task

EXAMPLE

The Weekly Planning Worksheet

PRIORITIES	THIS WEEK'S STEPS OF ACTION
Area One Myself	- Exercise five times this week; M/T/W/Th/Sat. - Make an appointment to see my doctor.
Area Two My Family	- Take my wife/husband/partner out to dinner on Friday. - Get a sitter. - Plan a family trip to the zoo.
Area Three Recruit Top Talent	- Set up interviews with top candidates.
Area Four Rehire My Best People Every Day	- Place birthdays of team members in my calendar. - Purchase personalized thank you cards for quick notes to team members. Write two.
Area Five Build Internal Relationships	- Contact HR department head and schedule her/him to come in and speak to our team.
Area Six Excel at Coaching Team Members	- Schedule one-on-one review sessions with each team member for the next month. - Conduct one hour-long review session this week.

© 2007 Leadership Link, Inc.

The Weekly Planning Worksheet

PRIORITIES	THIS WEEK'S STEPS OF ACTION
Area One	
Area Two	
Area Three	
Area Four	
Area Five	
Area Six	

© 2007 Leadership Link, Inc.

* Fairley, Stephen, G and Zipp, William. **The Business Coaching Toolkit: Top 10 Strategies for Solving the Toughest Dilemmas Facing Organizations**. Hoboken, NJ: John Wiley & Sons, 2007.

The To Do List

<u>Things TO DO Today</u>

Date: _____   Completed Y/N:

1. _____   _____

2. _____   _____

3. _____   _____

4. _____   _____

5. _____   _____

6. _____   _____

7. _____   _____

8. _____   _____

9. _____   _____

10. _____   _____

11. _____   _____

12. _____   _____

13. _____   _____

14. _____   _____

15. _____   _____

16. _____   _____

Hint for Success: Only place on this list the things you can REALISTITICLY get done each day so you earn a sense of accomplishment when completed.

6 - Goal Setting

Goal setting is a powerful process for thinking about your ideal future, both in your professional and your personal life, as well as for motivating yourself to turn your vision of this future into reality. The process of setting goals helps you choose where you want to go in your world.

Below is a sample methodology for setting business goals. Use it or find one that you like and implement it. Goal setting will help give you clarity of mind to get where you want to go.

Business Coaching Exercise:

Making Goals SMART*

A Business Case for Better Goals

Goals don't work for the following reasons:

- Goals by Themselves Do Not Provide Context

    - Context is critical to Goal setting.

    - A goal that is set without understanding the bigger picture of overall business objectives and fundamental priorities can ruin the organization.

- Goals Alone Do Not Bring Fulfillment

    - A **goal** gives us the _**how**_, but without a greater _**why**_ we lose our energy and endurance. With a _**how**_ we have a job; with a _**why**_ we have a cause. A **cause** is what ignites our passion and empowers us to act.

    - All goals need a **context**, the overall strategy in which they function, and a cause. There must be a set of underlying values it seeks to serve, a deeper _**why**_ to sustain the _**how**_. Goals alone do not supply these and do not work without them.

Better Goals are <u>SMART</u> Goals

S – Be <u>S</u>pecific

First, a SMART goal is specific. It says exactly what you want to do in clear, concrete terms. This is the fundamental difference between a wish and a goal. Wishes get us nowhere in business, but you would be surprised how many leaders fail at this first, fundamental point. While making a goal, SMART forces us to ask, "What is it exactly you want to do?" If the answer is, "I want to increase sales," this is not a goal; it is a wish. "I want a more positive work environment," also fails the SMART test. But if you said, "I want to reduce employee turnover by 25 percent," you now have the beginnings of a SMART goal.

M – Be <u>M</u>easurable

Second, a SMART goal is measurable. Measurement is often inherent in the specifics of the goal, but not always. You may want to increase customer satisfaction, but have no way of measuring it. A survey might work, a focus group, or even increased sales. To be SMART, a goal must land on means of measuring success and be trackable over time.

A – Be <u>A</u>chievable

Our goals must stretch us, yes, but the stretch must be reasonable and balanced with other priorities.

Talk with others about the feasibility of your goals. Look at industry standards and reflect on the accomplishments of those who have gone before you.

R – Be <u>R</u>elevant

Relevant goals must be in line with overall business objectives.

Relevance is the key to sustained goal fulfillment. We won't accomplish something over time tat we are not internally committed to with all our heart. Again, goals are our servants, not our masters, and must serve the greater purpose of our values and priorities to truly be SMART.

T – Be <u>T</u>ime Bound

Finally, if you don't have a deadline, you don't have a goal. The specifics of the goal must answer the question, "By when?"

Intermediate time targets, called milestones, can also be set for your goal. Milestones keep a person on track with reasonable progress toward the finish line.

Business Coaching Exercise: The SMART Goal Worksheet

Here is a five-step system for setting goals that work.

1. State Your Goal in One Sentence and Make it **SMART**

2. List the Main Benefits of Achieving This Goal

3. List the Steps of Action for Achieving This Goal

4. List the Possible Obstacles for the Completion of This Goal

5. List the Possible Solutions to the Obstacles of This Goal

SMART GOAL WORKSHEET

Name: John Jones	**Date:** Feb. 2, 2016

SMART Goal (Specific, Measurable, Relevant, Time bound)

To achieve $1.8 million of agricultural sales in 2007 by selling $600K of fertilizer by April, $600K of fungicide and growth regulator by June, and $600K of lime, herbicide, and other products by December.

BENEFITS of Achieving this Goal

I will feel a great sense of accomplishment of having sold more product than in any other year.
I will feel good about the job I am doing for my company; a place where I enjoy working.
I will enjoy increased pay through commissions and bonuses.
I will set the table for years of repeat business with these customers.

STEPS of ACTION for Achieving this Goal

1. Update and analyze soil samples of all my customers by February 24.
2. Write up fertilizer blend recommendations based on soil samples by March 8.
3. Make appointments with all my customers to present recommendations by March 10.
4. Apply first round of dry fertilizer by March 30.
5. Apply second round of liquid fertilizer by April 30.

Possible OBSTACLES	Possible SOLUTIONS
1. Letting a bottleneck develop by doing all of my own soil sample work.	1. Work closely with scouts to help with gathering soil samples.
2. Losing sales due to pricing concerns.	2. Get pricing strategy set before customers bring it up.
3. Losing sales due to product supply.	3. Solve the problem at management level.

How Many SMART Goals Should a Person Work on at One Time?

How many goals should you have? Less is more. I recommended focusing on two, at the most three, SMART goals at one time. Beyond that I have observed that a person gets overwhelmed and performance diminish.

GOAL WORKSHEET

Name:	**Date:**

SMART Goal (Specific, Measurable, Relevant, Time bound)

BENEFITS of Achieving this Goal

STEPS of ACTION for Achieving this Goal

Possible OBSTACLES	**Possible SOLUTIONS**

*Fairley, Stephen, G and Zipp, William. **The Business Coaching Toolkit: Top 10 Strategies for Solving the Toughest Dilemmas Facing Organizations**. Hoboken, NJ: John Wiley & Sons, 2007.

How to Make Decisions

All of us have to make decisions every day.

Some decisions, like, "Is this report ready to send to my boss now?" are relatively straightforward and simple. While others, such as, "Which of these candidates should I select for the job?" can be quite complex.

Simple decisions usually need a simple decision-making process. But difficult decisions typically involve issues like these:

- **Uncertainty** – Many facts may not be known.
- **Complexity** – You have to consider many interrelated factors.
- **High-risk consequences** – The impact of the decision may be significant.
- **Alternatives** – Each has its own set of uncertainties and consequences.
- **Interpersonal issues** – It can be difficult to predict how other people will react.

With these difficulties in mind, the best way to make a complex decision is to use an effective process. Clear processes usually lead to consistent, high-quality results, and they can improve the quality of almost everything we do. In this article, we outline a process that will help improve the quality of your decisions.

A Systematic Approach to Decision Making

A logical and systematic decision-making process helps you address the critical elements that result in a good decision. By taking an organized approach, you're less likely to miss important factors, and you can build on the approach to make your decisions better and better.

There are six steps to making an effective decision:

1. Create a constructive environment.

2. Generate good alternatives.

3. Explore these alternatives.

4. Choose the best alternative.

5. Check your decision.

6. Communicate your decision, and take action.

Key Points

An organized and systematic decision-making process usually leads to better decisions. Without a well-defined process, you risk making decisions that are based on insufficient information and analysis. Many variables affect the final impact of your decision. However, if you establish strong foundations for decision making, generate good alternatives, evaluate these alternatives rigorously, and then check your decision-making process, you will improve the quality of your decisions.

8 – Problem Solving

Whether you're solving a problem for a customer, supporting those who are solving problems, or discovering new problems to solve, the problems you face can be large or small, simple or complex, and easy or difficult. A fundamental part of every business is finding ways to solve them.

Some problems are easy to solve and some are more complex and complicated to solve. Below is a business industry standard method to solve more sophisticated problems. If your problem is big enough, it may merit a **S-W-O-T Analysis.** Again, don't be overwhelmed by this information use it if you need it, but I suspect as your business grows, you will have a problem that will warrant this type of analysis.

S-W-O-T Analysis *

SWOT stands for Strengths, Weaknesses, Opportunities and Threats. It is a way of summarizing the current state of a company and helping to devise a plan for the future, one that employs the existing strengths, redresses existing weaknesses, exploits, opportunities and defends against threats.

A New Twist on SWOT

	Internal Reality	External Reality
Positive	Strengths	Opportunities
Negative	Weaknesses	Threats

Below is a sample of a **S-W-O-T** analysis in action. Change the questions to the problem you are experiencing at the time. The questions don't have to be complicated or sophisticated just a means to expose as many issues as possible before you make a business decision.

Strengths

1. What do clients and outside partners say is your top strength?

_____

_____

_____

2. What do you currently do better than anyone else?

_____

_____

_____

3. What were your motivating factors and influences in starting this business or taking this leadership role?

_____

_____

_____

4. What achievements have you found the most satisfaction in doing?

_____

_____

_____

5. To what do you attribute your current level of success?

_____

_____

_____

6. How do you measure success? What does success look like to you?

_____

_____

_____

7. What are the top five reasons a client should buy from you and not the competitors?

_____

_____

_____

8. What are the top five reasons a company should hire or promote you?

_____

_____

_____

9. What are two real-life examples where you or your team showed creativity and ingenuity?

_____

_____

_____

10. What are two real-life examples where you or your team demonstrated critical thinking and were open-minded to trying new ways?

_____

_____

_____

Weaknesses

1. What are two or three areas your staff or team members complain about the most?

_____

_____

_____

2. What are two or three areas your clients or customers complain about the most?

_____

_____

_____

3. Of the following areas, which ones do you do the poorest in: customer follow-up, timely billing, marketing, sales, being detailed oriented, customer satisfaction, empowering team members to make decisions, and so forth?

_____

_____

_____

4. What does your competition do better than you??

_____

_____

_____

5. Which areas do you, your employees, or partners procrastinate the most on?

_____

_____

_____

6. How do you position your company in comparison to your competitor? (The cheapest, most expensive, generalist, specialist, small, big, focused, diverse, and so on.)

_____

_____

_____

7. What do clients and outside partners say is your top strength?

_____

_____

_____

Opportunities

1. Who are the people who already have a relationship with your potential clients? How can you start to build a relationship with them?

_____

_____

_____

2. What are you doing to position your company as being on the cutting edge as a leader in the industry?

_____

_____

_____

3. How could you better use the media to position yourself and your company as experts?

_____

_____

_____

4. How could you take full advantage of:

- Changes in technology (for example, online social networking websites, blogs, auto-responders, e-commerce, outsourcing)

- Changes to the marketplace, both locally and nationally

- Changes in social patterns, population movement, changing demographics, lifestyle changes, and so on

- Changes in buying cycles and needs (faster turnaround time, lower prices, more selection, better quality, customization requests, and so on)

_____

_____

_____

_____

_____

_____

_____

_____

_____

_____

Threats

1. What are the five greatest obstacles your company or team currently faces?

_____

_____

_____

2. How does rapidly changing technology affect your business model?

_____

_____

_____

3. What are the current trends in your industry?

_____

_____

_____

4. How does the economy affect your business for good or bad?

_____

_____

_____

5. What are you currently doing to identify, train, and retain your top employees?

_____

_____

_____

6. What would happen if your top three people were hired away by your most aggressive competitor?

_____

_____

_____

7. How long would it take you to be up and running if your company was robbed or your building burned down?

_____

_____

_____

8. What is the worst-case scenario you fear the most?

_____

_____

_____

9. How can you better prepare to minimize the damage this would cause if it ever came true?

_____

_____

_____

Questions for Deeper SWOT Analysis

The following four questions are best used after you have already answered the earlier questions because they are based on comparing and contrasting two areas of the SWOT grid to determine different strategies needed for success.

1. How can your strengths be leveraged to take advantage of developing opportunities? What are the strengths you will need to develop in the next 12 to 24 months to better position yourself or your company to profit from and quickly take advantage of new opportunities as they arise? **This is an S-O analysis, the upper tier of the SWOT grid of Strengths and Opportunities.**

2. What specific ways can your strengths be used to counteract potential threats? How can you create an environment such that your team's creative thinking, ingenuity, and exceptional follow-through can flourish and not be diluted by perceived or real threats? **This is an S-T analysis, a cross tier of the SWOT grid of Strengths and Threats.**

3. How can your weaknesses be overcome to tap into developing opportunities? What additional opportunities could you benefit from if you didn't have these weaknesses? What are two ways you could use delegation, outsourcing, or technology to minimize or eliminate your weaknesses? **This is called a W-O analysis, a cross tier of the SWOT grid of Weaknesses and Opportunities.**

4. Can you change your weaknesses by adding to or changing your team so that you can quickly counteract real threats? How does your team decide whether something is a real threat versus a perceived threat? How can you empower your team to take decisive action, instead of being paralyzed, in the face of a real threat? **This is called a W-T analysis, the bottom tier of the SWOT grid of Weaknesses and Threats.**

	Internal Reality	**External Reality**
Positive	Strengths	Opportunities
Negative	Weaknesses	Threats

* Fairley, Stephen, G and Zipp, William. **The Business Coaching Toolkit: Top 10 Strategies for Solving the Toughest Dilemmas Facing Organizations**. Hoboken, NJ: John Wiley & Sons, 2007.

9 – Delegation

Delegation is the assignment of responsibility to another person to carry out specific activities. It is one of the core concepts of management leadership. The person who delegated the work still remains accountable for the outcome of the delegated work. Delegation in the beginning may be difficult and/or not an option. In time, however, you will find that you will not be able to perform all the tasks necessary in your business. As you are the face of your business, in the beginning, customers will want to interact with you directly. Furthermore, the priority of any business is to generate revenues. Though the "back office" work is important and necessary to get done, it is the revenue generation that allows that to happen. Everything starts with the "closing the deal". If there are no deals closed there is no revenue. And if there is no revenue it does not really matter how good your back office works or doesn't work.

Below is a business tool to help you with delegation. With all tools "use what you like and leave the rest". Having business tools is starting point in your business. Some tools seem practical and others may seem over the top while other tools need to be customized to your specific needs. It's better to have more tools than less because you never know when I business situation may arise that you are not prepared for yet you have a tool to help you solve the problem which may be the difference in winning or losing a deal.

<u>Getting Things Done Through Others</u>
(Delegation Tool)

PAR: A New Approach to Delegation*

The secret to getting things done through others is having a system that allows both freedom and accountability. This system must be able to clarify expectations up front and provide opportunity for input from those involved in completing the task. There must also be flexibility in the system to allow for midcourse corrections, reworking the plans if necessary. That is the system we propose here captured in the acronym **PAR**.

<u>P – Plan</u>   <u>A – Act with Authority</u>   <u>R – Review</u>

The Cycle of Delegation

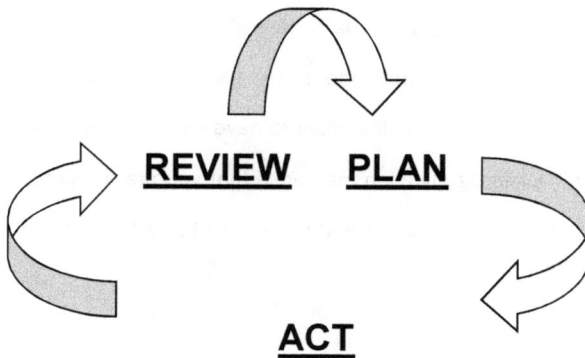

<u>REVIEW</u>   <u>PLAN</u>

<u>ACT</u>

The PAR Delegation Flow Chart

P Plan	Co-create a **PLAN** for the task or project, setting clear Expectations **in writing** by answering these four questions: **WHO?**　　　**WHAT?**　　　**WHEN?**　　　**HOW?** is going to do　　　by　　　　and　　　(and not how)
A Act with Authority	Free this person or group to **ACT with AUTHORITY** within a specified time frame, being available if needed. **AUTHORITY LEVELS:**　　Information　　Collaboration　　Execution **TIMEFRAME TO COMPLETE TASK(S)** **1**　　　　**2**　　　　**3**　　　　**4** week/month　weeks/months　weeks/months　weeks
R Review	Take time to **REVIEW** execution of the plan by asking three questions, making any necessary midcourse corrections. **PROGRESS?**　　**PROBLEMS?**　　**PLANS?** The Past　　　The Present　　The Future

The PAR Delegation Worksheets

P - Plan

Task/Project Name: _____

Expectations: _____

_____

_____

WHO?: _____

_____

_____

WHAT?: _____

_____

_____

WHEN?: _____

HOW?: _____

_____

_____

OR NOT HOW?: _____

_____

_____

The PAR Delegation Worksheets

<u>A – Act with Authority</u>

WHO?: _____

WHAT?: _____

AUTHORITY
LEVELS: Information   Collaboration   Execution

TIMEFRAME TO COMPLETE TASK(S)

1	**2**	**3**	**4**
week/month	weeks/months	weeks/months	weeks

WHO?: _____

WHAT?: _____

AUTHORITY
LEVELS: Information   Collaboration   Execution

TIMEFRAME TO COMPLETE TASK(S)

1	**2**	**3**	**4**
week/month	weeks/months	weeks/months	weeks/months

WHO?: _____

WHAT?: _____

AUTHORITY
LEVELS: Information   Collaboration   Execution

TIMEFRAME TO COMPLETE TASK(S)

1	**2**	**3**	**4**
week/month	weeks/months	weeks/months	weeks/months

The PAR Delegation Worksheets
<u>R - Review</u>

WHO?: _____

WHAT?: _____

PROGRESS?: _____
The Past

_____

_____

_____

PROBLEMS?: _____
The Present

_____

_____

_____

PLANS?: _____
The Future

_____

_____

_____

MORE ON GETTING THINGS DONE THROUGH OTHERS

- Begin with the WHO

- Help your WHO become His/Her Best

- Track the Things You Delegate

- Make Your Checkpoint Meetings Short

* Fairley, Stephen, G and Zipp, William. **The Business Coaching Toolkit: Top 10 Strategies for Solving the Toughest Dilemmas Facing Organizations**. Hoboken, NJ: John Wiley & Sons, 2007.

10 - The Toolkit at www.MindTools.com

A website I would like to recommend is **www.MindTools.com**. MindTools.com teaches you the leadership, team management, problem-solving, personal productivity, and team-working skills that you need for a successful business/career. I suggest that you start with their free tools, which you can learn about on their website. If you find these useful, then subscribe to their free e-Newsletter. And, for the full Mind Tools career development experience, try their Mind Tools Club.

You can learn hundreds of useful business/career skills for free by visiting their **Toolkit** page, or by using the menu on all information pages. And by subscribing to their free e-Newsletter, you'll learn new business management and career techniques every week. This helps you make professional and personal development an ongoing part of your life, keeping your skills fresh and up-to-date.

D. Personal Life

1 - Plan your personal life the way you plan your professional life

Do not lose perspective on all parts of your life. It is very healthy to have a good "work life balance". In your business calendar, you should be planning your personal life "to do's" the same way you plan your professional (business) "to do's". By doing this it insures that they will be attended to and completed. Life has a way of passing us by if we don't make time for the important things and people in our lives, both on a professional level and on a personable level.

2 – Have Fun! ☺

Another thing, have fun doing all of these stuff. The amount of work can be daunting at times. Make your professional and personal days enjoyable! One nice thing about working for yourself is that you control your time. Every so often, take a long lunch, make a Tuesday afternoon and make it Saturday afternoon instead, and make time for yourself after a major or even minor accomplishment. We all know what hard work looks like, but there is also a need to know what fun and relaxation looks like as well. Remember it's **always about balance**; too much of anything tends to put one out of balance. If you are going to work hard you might as well play hard as well! ☺

NOTES

Chapter 3: Your Life's Purpose...What's it all About Alfie?

Since the beginning of humankind, after man's search for food, lodging and procreation, he/she started wondering – What am I doing here? What is the purpose of my existence? Should I be doing something in particular with my life? These questions and many more have been concerning humankind for eons, so why should today, in this time and this place be any different?

Your journey, should you decide to accept it (and I hope that you do ☺), is to find your life purpose. It may be challenging at times, in so many different ways, to discover your life purpose, however, it is inside you nevertheless. It is truly a process of discovery. It is a process of discovering your real self, your true self, the self that is you in this time and in this place. The process will challenge you in ways known and unknown to you; but I will guarantee you, once you have found your life's purpose, your life's true mission, you will never be the same again! Your life will be elevated to a whole new level – one of joy, peace and prosperity!

This chapter will give you all the necessary tools you need to discover and implement your life's purpose. Some of the tools may not be new to you, while others will open your perception in a whole new way. Other methods, tools and techniques will take you to places you have never been before. You will be learning new things, re-learning not so new things and be opening up your mind, body and spirit to the most wonderful adventure of your life! The journey to your life's purpose! The journey to discovering why you are really here!

We will be discussing the tangible and intangible aspects of discovering your life's purpose. **We will start with the creative and end up with the concrete.** This resource is designed to give you "practical and proven" tools for you to discover, achieve and live your life's purpose. This book or I should call it a "Lifebook" has tools, methods and techniques that are used in the "real" world to help you make a living once you have discovered your life's purpose and achieve all the prosperity you need, want and desire.

You have chosen wisely on discovering your life's purpose. Now enjoy the adventure of growing, knowing, learning and achieving all that you can be! Let the fun, joy and adventure begin now...

Why Are We Here On This Beautiful Planet?

In certain parts of this chapter, I would ask that you be open minded. I would ask that you be "open to the possibility of…". I would ask you to suspend your belief system for a short while and be open to a new way of thinking; this chapter is just one of these areas that I would ask you to do so.

I would ask you to think about the true meaning of life, the true meaning of *your* life. And though this has been a question that has been pondered and discussed for millennia, it is just as fresh and relative **now** as it was then. The purpose of asking this question is to open one's mind to understand that we as individuals are part of a whole.

What whole is that you ask? The whole of this planet, the whole of all of humankind; even I dare say, the whole of the Universe and in being part of this whole, this means that each one of us has a unique role in this whole. And, that unique role is performing **"our work"** and our true work is unique to each of us. Let's go a step further with these concepts.

What if this planet is "a classroom" or "a community" of some type; and in this classroom or community, we are here to learn certain lessons of sorts, maybe even call them "life lessons" and do our work? **What if** these life lessons were meant to help us grow as individuals, to become better people, better human beings and help others grow as well? **What if** this was all true? How would you live your life? What would you do and what would you **not** do?

Whatever your beliefs are, do you think the above is possible? Do you think it applies to all of us? Do you think you would live your life differently? By the time we finish our time together this entire section will have a different perspective for you.

Let's spend a little time exploring some of these questions; the answers will help you find your life's true purpose.

Exercise: Answer these questions to the best of your ability. There are no right or wrong answers. Just ponder these areas and be open to the possibilities.

1. What do you think is the meaning of life?

_____

_____

_____

_____

2. What do you think is the meaning of **your** life?

_____

_____

_____

_____

3. Do you think we/you are here on this planet at this time and in this place for a specific reason?

_____

_____

_____

_____

4. Do you believe we are part of a whole? Why or why not?

_____

_____

_____

_____

Being Human – What Does It Really Mean?

We human beings are made up of four components.

1.   The Physical (of the Body)

2.   The Mental (of the Mind)

3.   The Emotional (of the Heart)

4.   The Spiritual (of the Life Force within Us).

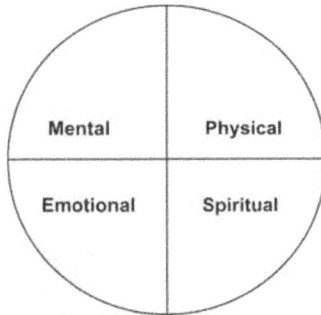

These 4 components are **interdependent** upon one another. What happens to one component has an impact on the other components. **Each of the components has a function of its own and together they comprise a human being or the attributes of "being human".**

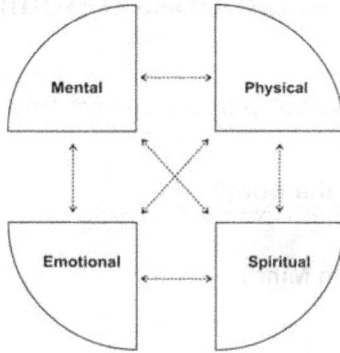

Mental   Physical

Emotional   Spiritual

If any of these four components are out of balance, we experience **"dis-ease"**. When we experience "dis-ease" in the body, it becomes sickness. When in the mind it becomes a mental illness of sorts. In the heart, it becomes "heart ache" or an emotional disorder. In the spiritual, it is viewed as being "spiritually disconnected".

To achieve optimum wellness, each component needs to be kept free from "dis-ease". This is achieved by exercising each area.

The Physical is exercised through the body by feeding it proper nourishment, performing proper physical activity, and keeping away from anything deemed "poisons" to the body.

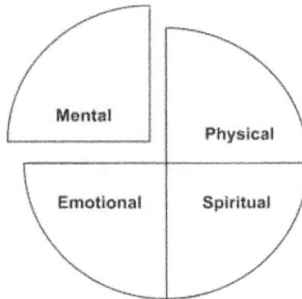

The Mental is exercised by **positive** reading, viewing **positive** events, doing **positive** visualizations and, placing **positive** things into the mind.

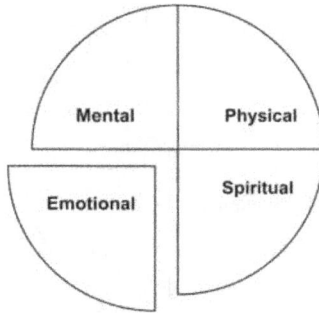

The Emotional is exercised by demonstrating acts of service, love; for self, for those close to us and all humankind. Basically, being of service to others.

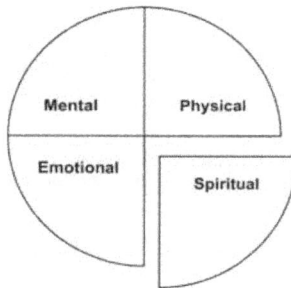

The Spiritual is exercised by **meditation** on one's connection to Nature, the Universe, the Source, The Creator, God.

In seeking your life's purpose you will find that all of the above components (physical, mental, emotional and spiritual) of your life need to be in balance. For what good will it do you when you find your true work and attain the prosperity you desire if you are physically ill, mentally exhausted, emotionally drained and not connected spiritually. **How can you have a fulfilling life if you have any "dis-ease" going on?**

It is so important to have the proper balance in your life in all the four areas; **Physically** – to eat right and exercise, **Mentally** – to think good thoughts and put good things into one's mind, **Emotionally** – to open one's heart to a healthy love of one's self and to love others and **Spiritually** – to make and keep conscious contact with your Higher Power, whatever that may mean to you, be it God, the Universe, nature, humankind.

As discussed earlier, when we get out of balance in any areas of our lives, we experience "dis-ease" and this dis-ease can and will affect our work and our life purpose. That is why being in balance and staying in balance is so important. For those of us who have found our work it is important that we are good examples to help those that are seeking their work and purpose. This does not mean we are to be perfect for we all are human and must deal with the trials and tribulations of being such; however, we should do our best to strive to be in balance to the best of our abilities.

Exercise: Answer these questions to the best of your ability. There are no any rights or wrong answers. Just ponder these areas and be open to the possibilities.

1. What happens to you when you are out of balance – physically, mentally, emotionally and spiritually?

_____

_____

_____

_____

2. What can you do to get back into balance – physically, mentally, emotionally and spiritually?

_____

_____

_____

_____

Some Exercises To Make Your Creativity Flow!

I repeated this section, for many people it may be a new way of thinking, using your mind and exploring one's own abilities. The times have changed and you need to be comfortable speaking about all your education (formal and/or informal) and skill sets (professional training, on the job and/or self-taught). In essence, one must learn to **"bang your own drum"** without sounding conceded or arrogant, but in a gracious and confident manner.

The following easy exercises are meant to center you physically, mentally, emotionally and spiritually. None of these exercises are difficult. You will soon observe the positive benefits of these methods and techniques. **Although none of the following exercises are strenuous. As with any new exercise program, you may want to check with your doctor before you begin.**

The main benefit of these exercises is to help your creativity flow as well as having you achieve balance in your life as we spoke about in the previous chapter. When we have balance in our lives everything seems to flow with ease and grace. When we are out of balance, things become much more of a struggle.

Perform these exercises on a daily basis. Just do what feels right to you. There is no need for stress or strain as there is no need to reach a specific goal. **It is always about progress and not perfection.**

Exercise - Breathing for Relaxation

Taking deep **s-l-o-w** breaths in and out will help you relax.

The benefit of this exercise is to help one become calm, peaceful and centered.

8. Take a slow, deep **breath in** for a count up to four – one, two, three, four.

9. Then slowly **exhale out** for a count up to four – one, two, three, four.

10. Take a slow, deep **breath in** for a count up to four – one, two, three, four.

11. Then slowly **exhale out** for a count up to four – one, two, three, four.

12. Take a slow, deep **breath in** for a count up to four – one, two, three, four.

13. Then slowly **exhale out** for a count up to four – one, two, three, four.

14. Perform this exercise 3 or 4 times and notice how relaxed you become.

You can do this exercise as often as you like.

<u>DO NOT</u> DO THESE EXERCISES WHILE DRIVING.

Exercise - Clear Your Mind

This exercise helps you clear your mind. For example, when you are thinking about too many things or are on "mind overload".

The benefit is to help you be calm, relax and think clearly.

1. Sit comfortably in a quiet environment.

2. Close your eyes and slowly begin to breathe deeply to a count of four (1 – 2 – 3 – 4).

3. Mentally focus on the word - **RELAX**.

4. If other thoughts enter your mind, gently bring your attention back to the word – **RELAX**.

5. Calmly, breathe and do it again.

6. Continue for a few minutes.

7. Open your eyes and stretch – inhale and exhale fully.

You can do this exercise as often as you like.

<u>DO NOT</u> DO THESE EXERCISES WHILE DRIVING.

Exercise - Visualization for Your Life Purpose

Visualization refers to the practice of seeking to affect the outer world by changing one's thoughts. You can choose to visualize anything you desire in life, including your life purpose. You may want to record this exercise and play it back to yourself.

The benefit of this exercise is to help you create an environment that can help you visualize your life purpose.

1. Find a place that is quiet and you will not be disturbed. Now close your eyes and take a nice deep breath. Take a nice deep, deep breath. Relax your mind; relax your body. You are totally calm and totally relaxed; totally calm and totally relaxed.

2. Count from four down to the number one. With every number you count, I would like you to take a deep breath, and each time say the word "relax," Relax and exhale the breath from your body. With every number you count, take a deep breath, and each time say the word "relax", relax and allow the breath to exhale from your body.

Four, take a nice deep breath (pause) and relax.

Three, take a nice deep breath (pause) and relax.

Two, take a nice deep, deep breath (pause) and relax.

One, deep breath (pause)… and relax. Relax your thoughts; relax your body.

Very good, now continue to breathe normally.

3. Now count from four down to one again. Mentally release each group of muscles that is called to your attention.

Four, release the muscles in the head and face. Just release and relax. Feel your head slowly drop forward if that is comfortable for you.

Three, release the muscles in your neck and shoulders. Just release and relax any stress and any strain.

 Two, release the muscles in your back and allow your hands to fall to your sides if you wish.

One, release the muscles in your stomach and feel the relaxation flow down through your legs and feet.

Like a series of dominoes, all the muscles in your body begin at the top of your head and flow into one another as each one releases and relaxes.

With every beat of your heart, with every breath that you take, you will become more relaxed, calmer, more relaxed, calmer...

... Good. Continue to use your imagination. Imagine the warm, golden sun going down into your skin and melting deeply within every cell of your body.

     4.   The gentle warmth flows over through your muscles, allowing them to relax. Release and relax all of the tension; all of the strain.

Feel the muscles in your neck and shoulders expand.

Notice how you feel - without stress - free in your body and mind. Your heart rate and breathing are calm and relaxed. Your muscles are totally relaxed. Totally calm, totally relaxed. Totally calm, totally relaxed.

     5.   Now, think about a time in the **future**. In a vision, see yourself living your life's purpose. What type working are you doing? Where are you doing it? With what type of people? Are there any specific smells? Use all of your senses. See it. Touch it. Experience it! Just let it come to you...

     6.   See yourself living your life's purpose. Being happy, fulfilled, prosperous, you are full of joy and wonderment. So happy doing your work!

     7.   When I count to four... you will be wide awake...feeling good and alert. Remembering everything you experienced in your visualization and able to write it down if you wish....One...you're beginning to come back...Two... feel the energy start flowing through your body...Three... moving your fingers and toes... more and more awake...feel the energy running through your body ...Four... breathing in wakeful energy... clearing your head... balancing your energies... feeling wonderful in every way..., opening your eyes... fully coming back... fully back... wide awake... and ready to go...

You can do this exercise once a day.
You can do it more if you like.

<u>DO NOT</u> DO THESE EXERCISES WHILE DRIVING.

What's Your Passion?

In this section, we are going to throw reality out the window for a short time. What is your passion? What do you really love to do? If someone were to say to you, I will pay you a very good salary/fee for your services, what would that service be? This is a very good time to start "brainstorming" with yourself and others about what you are really passionate about. Money is no object! **This chapter is about your emotions.** What makes you happy! ☺ Give this some time and sit with these concepts. Use the creative exercises in previous chapters to help you get started. There are no right or wrong answers here. It is a place to think out loud, a laboratory of sorts.

Why is this important you may ask? Sometimes we have a habit of only thinking in a certain way, and we need to stir things up a bit! If you are a conventional thinking person be unconventional here! If you are an unconventional thinking person try some conventional thinking for a change. If you are an analytical thinking person, get creative and conversely, if you are a creative person, think analytically. Use both sides of your brain. **Think out of the box; think out of _your_ box.** You will be pleasantly surprised!

Exercise:

1. What do you love to do?

_____

_____

_____

_____

2. Why do you like doing it?

_____

_____

_____

_____

3. What education and skills did you need to do your passion?

_____

_____

_____

_____

How Would You Like To Live Your Life?

As an extension of what was discussed in the previous section, what specifically would you like to do with your life? Now this may involve some research to learn about different careers, jobs and vocations. **When doing your research make sure you copy down the required skills and education to do that specific job, it's very important if you should you choose to go in that direction.**

You may want to be a doctor but after you research the skills and education required, it may not be the right thing for you to do. **HOWEVER,** you may like or want to be a healer of some type, explore other modalities of healing, i.e.; becoming a nurse or maybe something in the holistic healing arts. There are many holistic healing modalities to choose.

The research you do here will service you well, as it will help you get clarity on what you would like or not like to do as your work. **The reality is, once you do discover what your work is, there will be certain skills and education required and you will need to know what they are to enable you to get the required background to do your true work.**

Exercise:

1. What would you love to do with your life? Forget about boundaries and just go for it!

_____

_____

_____

_____

_____

2. What are the required skills and education you need to do your work?

_____

_____

_____

_____

3. In the table below identify the title, skills and education you need and keep this as your "short list" for your potential work?

Title	Skills	Education
Example:		
Restaurant Chef	Cooking Skills	Cooking School

NOTES

Finding Your Path As To Where You Want To Go

Once you have given some thought as to what you feel your work is, then comes the task of understanding the reality of getting to that point. Does it require more education, or more skills or more experience and/or all of the above? In order to do your work these items need to be addressed. Do take heart! Say your work is to be a healer and initially your research brought you to the conclusion that you want to become a doctor. After researching the reality of becoming a doctor, i.e.; the schooling, the time required, and the financial commitment required, you come to the conclusion that it is not practical in your world. **You can still do your work as a healer.** The healing arts are so varied that you will find your path and your work. In the healing arts alone, there are many paths one can take. Keep in mind that you may start on one healing path only to find yourself settling into another modality and still performing your true work.

This chapter is here to assist you in getting some clarity on the specific skills, education and experience you will need to perform your work. Once again, be open to the possibility of your work coming to you in different ways. It may be a traditional role like a medical doctor or a non-traditional one as a Reiki Master. Both flow the energy of a healer and both help people achieve wellness.

Exercise:

1. Investigate what it would take to get to where you want to go.

_____

_____

_____

_____

_____

_____

_____

_____

_____

_____

_____

2. Write down your skills. Don't be modest and take nothing for granted. Skills are anything you know how to do, you are good at doing it and you can do it again.

Skill	Details About Skill Acquired
Example:	
Cooking skills	Was a short order cook at a marina in the summer.

3. Write down your education. This is both formal education and informal education. Formal education like degrees and certificates and informal education like on the job training and self-education. Here again don't be modest.

Date	Education	Subject Matter	Institution	Comments
Example:				
11/12/2013	Certificate	Cooking	Local High School	Learned cooking basics
11/20/2013	Self-taught	Baking	Home	Baked cookies from book

4. Write down your life experience relative to what you are interested in doing. Take nothing for granted as it may be an important aspect of your true work.

_____

_____

_____

_____

_____

_____

_____

_____

_____

_____

_____

_____

What Are Your Attributes, Personal Gifts and Talents and?

What would you say are your natural gifts, things that just come easily to you? Are you a talented speaker, good with people; are you a good cook, good with your hands? We all have gifts, what are yours? What do people compliment you about? You can recycle some of the things mentioned in previous chapters, however, given this some deep thought. Use the meditation exercise to really ponder and reflect upon your naturally born gifts.

Exercise:

1. **Attributes** – What comes naturally to you? What is easy for you to do? Is it cooking, good with your hands, good with people?

Example: I'm good with people. Can get along with just about anyone.

_____

_____

_____

_____

_____

_____

_____

_____

_____

_____

2. **Personal Gifts** – We all have been given certain gifts or abilities. Do you have the gift of "gab" (being a good communicator)? Good with your hands? Very logical? Very Creative? Though similar to exercise 1, these are things that you just shine in doing.

Example: I'm able to speak with anyone on just about anything.

_____

_____

_____

_____

_____

_____

_____

_____

_____

3. Talents – Have you acquired and/or perfected certain talents or skills over the years. Are you naturally a talker and a good communicator? Have you developed the talent for professional public speaking, or have you developed the talent for writing? **Here, we are going from the general and honing into the specific.**

Example: I have become a professional public speaker thru training and practice.

_____

_____

_____

_____

_____

_____

_____

_____

_____

_____

Your Life Purpose Statement –
Let The World Know Who You Really Are!

What is your Life Purpose Statement?

Your Life Purpose Statement is similar to a company's Mission Statement in that you are telling others what your purpose is and how they can benefit from knowing and working with you. **This is done for a number of reasons, one of which is to inform people what you do and how it can help them.** We also live in a time that we need to let people know, in a short amount of time, what we do. This was evident when we speak about a networking introduction. In less than 2 minutes, which is the average attention span of an adult, you tell people who you are, what you do and how it can help them when you are looking for employment or looking for clients.

When we are talking about being of service and having others help us as well, if people don't understand what we do and how it can benefit them and others, how can you expect others to understand and refer you and your work? Though many people may feel uncomfortable speaking about themselves, the truth is, if you don't inform people about what you do and how it can benefit them, **you are doing a disservice** to both the people that need your help and yourself. I meet many nice people that think it is improper to talk about themselves, when in fact, they can be helping others that need and want their help. **There is a huge difference between informing people about what you do and how it can be of help to them and bragging about oneself.** The Life Purpose Statement, presented in a proper and professional manner, is just the tool to tell people what you do in a non-threatening way and helping yourself.

Sample Life Purpose Statements

The main thing to keep in mind is to tell people what you do and how it can benefit them and really what you are telling them is how it can benefit people in general. It does not have to be long - just informative. Think of your Life Purpose Statement as a conversation starter telling people in a short and precise statement what you are all about. Once the conversation gets going then you can get into the details of what you do and how you do it. Your Life Purpose Statement is very similar to your networking introduction, similar tools used in different ways. The Life Purpose Statement just tells people what your work is without expecting anything in return. In the networking introduction, you are seeking to build relationship or find other contacts or whatever else is on your agenda.

Life Purpose Statements (Examples)

"As a **Life Purpose Coach** I help people find their purpose so they can perform their true work and lead happy, prosperous and fulfilled lives."

"As a **Corporate Philanthropic Analyst** I help people with my work by insuring my company makes wise and prudent decisions when sending our donations to help the right charities with their needs."

"As a **Baker** running my own business I help people gather together in my bakery where they can have a sense of community, talk, network and help one another with their needs."

"As a **Machinist** working in a factory I help people by performing quality work on the products I manufacture so people can enjoy their lives by using the products my company sells."

"As a **Mother/Father** I make sure that my children eat right, get the proper amount of exercise and rest, know the difference between right and wrong so they can help build a better future for everyone."

Exercise:

In this exercise you will be creating your Life Purpose Statement. First think about what you do, and then think about the benefits of what you do. Benefits are statements demonstrating how your services and/or products helps the person and/or people you are working with, as people always what to know what's in it for them.

What is/are the Service(s) and/or Product(s) to Deliver	What is/are the Benefits from this/these Product(s) and Service(s)
1. Life Purpose Coaching	1a. Help people achieve clarity as to their true life's work and purpose.
	1b. Help people lead happy, prosperous and fulfilled lives.
	1c. Help people with practical tools to make a living with their life purpose.
2.	2a.
	2b.
	2c.
3.	3a.
	3b.
	3c.
4.	4a.
	4b.
	4c.

Put it All Together Here

_____

_____

_____

_____

_____

_____

_____

_____

_____

_____

_____

_____

_____

_____

_____

_____

_____

_____

_____

_____

_____

Your Life Master Plan – Planning Your Work and Working Your Plan

What is a Life Master Plan and why should you write one?

A Life Master Plan simply stated is your blueprint to your goals, identifying how to achieve those goals and working those goals in realistic manner. This book gives you the tools, methods and techniques to discover and achieve your life purpose, now it's time to do some planning and then execution to achieve all your dreams, wants and desires. Your Life Master Plan does not need to be long or a drawn out dissertation just a few pages just to keep you on track as what you need to be doing to achieve your goals.

In **Section One** clearing define your goals. How many goals should you define? Start with between three and seven. You want to make goals realistic and achievable. What kind of goals should I be working on? What is important to you right now in your life? If you need clarity, remember the exercises you learned in the beginning of the book of breathing and meditation. **You want goals to be specific, measurable, achievable and realistic with a definitive time frame.** You also want your goals to be written, as writing and reading your goals makes them more realistic. For example, "I would like to lose 26 pounds or more in 6 months and will begin this goal starting January 1, 2016 and ending June 30, 2016". (**Always check with your doctor first when starting any weight loss program**). Notice how the goal fits the criteria mentioned above; **specific** – How much weight? – 26 pounds or more, **measurable** – At the end of the 6 months I will weigh myself and see how much weight I have lost, **achievable** – Doctor's advice not to lose not more than one or two pounds of weight each week and **realistic** – if I eat right and exercise it is an achievable goal **with a definitive time frame – 6 months (26 weeks).**

In **Section Two** identify the process as to what you need to have and what you need to do in order to achieve your goals. Do you need to have certain skills and education to achieve your goals? Do you have them? Need to acquire them? Do they need to be acquired in a specific order? Really think about at a high level what it takes to achieve that goal. Using the previous example of weight loss once again; "In order for me to lose weight I will have to change my diet and join a gym to exercise on a regular basis". So in order to achieve that goal it will mean an investment of time and money to lose the weight that I have as my goal.

In **Section Three** you need to create a working plan for the items you have identified in Section One and Section Two. This is the day-to-day operation of the plan. What will need to do on a day to day, week-to-week and/or month-to-month basis to execute and complete your plan? Let's use the example we have been using in the previous two sections for weight loss. "In order to achieve my goal of losing 26 pounds in 6 months I will eat a daily diet of lean protein meats, plenty of fresh fruits and vegetables, drink a quart of water each day and walk one mile each day". Once a month look at your plan and see what's working, what needs improvement and what needs to be changed.

Just a reminder, the Life Master Plan does not have to be long and drawn out document just a tool to keep you on track to your goals and if you get off your goals it is an easy way to get you back to achieving them. That's why you want to make your goals achievable for once you get the taste for success in achieving the first, second and third goal, there will be nothing standing in your way to achieve the life you desire. So start off small with goals that you can attain then work your way up to larger and more important goals.

Put It All Together Here

You Are Instilled with The Power to Manifest the Perfect Life Experience

The Law of Attraction

The Law of Attraction is one of the Universal Laws. Here is a brief explanation of Universal Laws. Universal Laws govern all creation. They are basic principles of life and have been around since the beginning of creation. They are laws of the Divine Universe. Universal Laws apply to everyone, everywhere. They cannot be changed. They cannot be broken.

The Law of Attraction is the most powerful law in the universe. It is simple in concept, but practice is necessary. Once you "get it", there is no looking back! It will always be a part of you. The simplest definition of this law is "like attracts like." Other definitions include: You get what you put your energy and focus on, whether wanted or unwanted. The Law of Attraction is neutral. All forms of matter and energy are attracted to that which is of a like vibration. You are a living magnet. Energy attracts like energy, "That which is like unto itself is drawn." Abraham-Hicks[1]

You can deliberately use this law to create your future!

Universal Law of Attraction

This universal law is working in your life right now, whether you are aware of it or not. You are attracting the people, situations, jobs and much more into your life. Once you are aware of this law and how it works, you can start to use it to deliberately attract what you want into your life.

How do you create your desires using the powerful law? There are just a few basic steps.

1. Ask

2. Source says YES!

3. Allow It

You must be very clear on exactly what your desire is. Focus on it. Give it all your positive energy. Visualize and raise your vibration about it. Feel good!

A major factor behind this Universal Law is the energy and vibrations of our emotions and feelings. Any thought you may have, when combined with emotion, vibrates out from you to the universe and will attract back what you want.

You can leave all the details to the Universe. Let the Universe figure out the method of delivery, when you will receive it, etc. Now all you have to do is allow It. Sounds easy, right? This can be the most difficult part to do. Be doubt-free. All you need to do is expect it. Act like you already have it. Be grateful.

And always take inspired action. If something feels right, then go ahead and do it. Taking action is an important step.

That is it! You can always be expectant of good things, your desires. Feel good knowing your desire is on its way to you.

Always Expect Your Desires. Expect Miracles.

Most of you who begin this deliberate creation beat up on yourselves too much and we would like to let you off the hook by saying to you that The Law of Attraction is a very powerful thing. And you can't fight the Law of Attraction. You just have to let the Law of Attraction play out as it will. So if you have a habit of thought, the Law of Attraction is going to bring more of that thought to you this means you're probably going to think that thought more. And as you think that thought more you're going to have more of those feelings and the Law of Attraction is going to bring you more of that stuff. It's sort of like being mad at gravity. Every time I jump in the air I come right down. And we say it helps to accept gravity. It helps to acknowledge that this is the way gravity works and in time you learn to deal with it. You learn that there are many more benefits to it than there are detriments. And the Law of Attraction is the same way. In time you come to realize its consistent nature is very beneficial to you so you don't ride around in the discomfort of the Law of Attraction, instead you let it work for you.[2]

Sample Creative Visualization Using Your Life Purpose

As mentioned in an earlier chapter Visualization refers to the practice of seeking to affect the outer world by changing one's thoughts. You can choose to visualize anything you desire in life, including your life purpose.

The benefit of this exercise is to help you create an environment that can help you visualize you living your life purpose.

1.   Find a place that is quiet and you will not be disturbed. Now close your eyes and take a nice deep breath. Take a nice deep, deep breath. Relax your mind; relax your body. You are totally calm and totally relaxed; totally calm and totally relaxed.

2.   Count from four down to the number one. With every number you count, I would like you to take a deep breath, and each time say the word "relax," Relax and exhale the breath from your body. With every number you count, take a deep breath, and each time say the word "relax", relax and allow the breath to exhale from your body.

Four, take a nice deep breath (pause) and relax.

Three, take a nice deep breath (pause) and relax.

Two, take a nice deep, deep breath (pause) and relax.

One, deep breath (pause)... and relax. Relax your thoughts; relax your body.

Very good, now continue to breathe normally.

3.   Now count from four down to one again. Mentally release each group of muscles that is called to your attention.

Four, release the muscles in the head and face. Just release and relax. Feel your head slowly drop forward if that is comfortable for you:

Three, release the muscles in your neck and shoulders. Just release and relax any stress and any strain.

Two, release the muscles in your back and allow your hands to fall to your sides if you wish.

One, release the muscles in your stomach and feel the relaxation flow down through your legs and feet.

Like a series of dominoes, all the muscles in your body begin at the top of your head and flow into one another as each one releases and relaxes.

With every beat of your heart, with every breath that you take, you will become more relaxed, calmer, more relaxed, calmer...

... Good. Continue to use your imagination. Imagine the warm, golden sun going down into your skin and melting deeply within every cell of your body.

4.   The gentle warmth flows over through your muscles, allowing them to relax. Release and relax all of the tension; all of the strain.

Feel the muscles in your neck and shoulders expand.

Notice how you feel - without stress - free in your body and mind. Your heart rate and breathing are calm and relaxed. Your muscles are totally relaxed. Totally calm, totally relaxed. Totally calm, totally relaxed.

5.   Now, think about a time in the **future**. In a vision, see yourself living your life's purpose. Meeting and helping people with your work. Maybe travelling, to the degree you desire. Fulfilling your true life purpose, your true work. You are happy knowing you are helping others, making a difference to their lives. See it. Touch it. Experience it! Use all of your senses.

6.   See yourself living your life's purpose. You are happy, fulfilled, and prosperous; you are full of joy and wonderment. So happy doing your work!

7.   When I count to four... you will be wide awake...feeling good and alert. Remembering everything you experienced in your visualization and able to write it down if you wish....One...you're beginning to come back...Two... feel the energy start flowing through your body...Three... moving your fingers and toes... more and more awake...feel the energy running through your body ...Four... breathing in wakeful energy... clearing your head... balancing your energies... feeling wonderful in every way..., opening your eyes... fully coming back... fully back... wide awake... and ready to go...

You can do this exercise once a day.
You can do it more if you like.

DO <u>NOT</u> DO THIS EXERCISE WHILE DRIVING.

Exercise:

Write your own visualization as to how you want to live your life purpose. You can use the previous visualization as a template as substitute your needs, wants and desires instead. Use sections 1, 2, 3, 4, 6, and 7 and just add your own section 5.

Creative Visualization Using <u>Your</u> Life Purpose

As mentioned in an earlier chapter Visualization refers to the practice of seeking to affect the outer world by changing one's thoughts. You can choose to visualize anything you desire in life, including your life purpose.

The benefit of this exercise is to help you create an environment that can help you visualize you living your life purpose.

1. Find a place that is quiet and you will not be disturbed. Now close your eyes and take a nice deep breath. Take a nice deep, deep breath. Relax your mind; relax your body. You are totally calm and totally relaxed; totally calm and totally relaxed.

2. Count from four down to the number one. With every number you count, I would like you to take a deep breath, and each time say the word "relax," Relax and exhale the breath from your body. With every number you count, take a deep breath, and each time say the word "relax", relax and allow the breath to exhale from your body.

Four, take a nice deep breath (pause) and relax.

Three, take a nice deep breath (pause) and relax.

Two, take a nice deep, deep breath (pause) and relax.

One, deep breath (pause)… and relax. Relax your thoughts; relax your body.

Very good, now continue to breathe normally.

3. Now count from four down to one again. Mentally release each group of muscles that is called to your attention.

Four, release the muscles in the head and face. Just release and relax. Feel your head slowly drop forward if that is comfortable for you.

Three, release the muscles in your neck and shoulders. Just release and relax any stress and any strain.

Two, release the muscles in your back and allow your hands to fall to your sides if you wish.

One, release the muscles in your stomach and feel the relaxation flow down through your legs and feet.

Like a series of dominoes, all the muscles in your body begin at the top of your head and flow into one another as each one releases and relaxes.

With every beat of your heart, with every breath that you take, you will become more relaxed, calmer, more relaxed, calmer...

... Good. Continue to use your imagination. Imagine the warm, golden sun going down into your skin and melting deeply within every cell of your body.

4. The gentle warmth flows over through your muscles, allowing them to relax. Release and relax all of the tension; all of the strain.

Feel the muscles in your neck and shoulders expand.

Notice how you feel - without stress - free in your body and mind. Your heart rate and breathing are calm and relaxed. Your muscles are totally relaxed. Totally calm, totally relaxed. Totally calm, totally relaxed.

5. Now, think about a time in the **future**. In a vision, see yourself living your life's purpose. Write your Life Purpose Statement here.

_____

_____

_____

_____

_____

_____

_____

6. See yourself living your life's purpose. You are happy, fulfilled, and prosperous; you are full of joy and wonderment. So happy doing your work!

7. When I count to four... you will be wide awake...feeling good and alert. Remembering everything you experienced in your visualization and able to write it down if you wish....One...you're beginning to come back...Two... feel the energy start flowing through your body...Three... moving your fingers and toes... more and more awake...feel the energy running through your body ...Four... breathing in wakeful energy... clearing your head... balancing your energies... feeling wonderful in every way..., opening your eyes... fully coming back... fully back... wide awake... and ready to go...

<u>DO NOT</u> DO THIS EXERCISE WHILE DRIVING.

Enjoy and Celebrate Your Life Purpose And Celebrate Your Life!

Celebrate Your Life Purpose!

Congratulations! You have discovered your life purpose and your true work. It has been a journey to get here and you finally made it! Now's it's time for a celebration! Do something good for yourself, go get a massage, spend a day at a spa, go spend some time with some of your favorite people. You've earned it!

On a more serious note, it is quite an achievement to have clearly defined your life purpose and have concrete steps to implement and live your life purpose to live a happier, prosperous and personally fulfilling life.

Be Good to Yourself - All You Need is Love...

Love - we all want it, yet how many people have it and are willing to give it away? It all starts with the individual loving oneself. Not physical love of the body, but love of the spirit. You must first have love for yourself, for how can you give away something to others that you do not have for yourself? We have love for other people, animals, inanimate objects and even food but do we have a healthy love of ourselves?

Love can be so misunderstood at times. Some people think of romantic love and others think of physical love. But can there be love just for love's sake? Can we love the person and not the body they inhabit? Of course we can. This is evident in all the major religions and their respective prophets, saints and angels. **Love is love.** When there is true love, a pure love, a real love, a healthy love, a love that transcends all space and time between two people who is to judge whether it is right or wrong? Only the Creator is to be that judge.

Love is Healing

The emotion of love is very strong. It can heal mind, spirit and some feel the body as well. It is a force so strong it cannot be denied. The love a parent has for a child transcends all space and all time. It is a love with no ending, even when the body is no longer here the love lives on. True love never dies.

Studies have shown that babies, who are not touched, do not develop properly, while those who are touched develop faster and are often discharged faster from the hospital. The power of love has the ability to heal on so many different levels. **Though we cannot see love we know it when we feel it.** The power of love transcends all. Love is a universal emotion in the world. Is the love of one's child different from someone who is rich versus someone who is poor? Is the love of one's child different for people of color, ethnic or religious backgrounds? Is the love one's child different in different parts of the world? No, it is not. **Love is love.**

The More You Give Love the More Love You Get

The funny thing about the gift of love is the more you give the more you get. It is though there is a natural law that you if give love you get more in return. Love is such a powerful emotion, yet why are so many people afraid to give love, show love, and receive love? The source of love is endless. You can give love and yet you will find even more love to give. It is an amazing emotion the Creator has given humankind; the gift of love.

So many gifts to humankind are free to give and yet priceless to receive. By demonstrating love to another person, both the giver and receiver are positively affected. Studies show the simple act of touching another, raises the serotonin level in the brain. Serotonin refers to a natural hormone that is produced by the body. Serotonin is produced in the pineal gland, which is part of the human brain. Research also suggests that touch deprivation in early development and again in adolescence may contribute to violence in adults. Further studies have found that a culture in which there was more physical affection toward young children had lower rates of adult physical violence, and vice versa. Furthermore, the amount of touching that occurs in different cultures is highly variable. Other studies have found that in the touching behavior in several countries, couples were observed sitting in cafes for 30-minute periods, and the amount of touching between them was recorded. Among the highest touch cultures was France (110 times per 30 minutes), while the U.S. was among the lowest (2 times per 30 minutes). Interestingly, high-touch cultures have relatively low rates of violence, and low-touch cultures have extremely high rates of youth and adult violence.

When your life is full of love you truly are prosperous indeed. Love has a way of making you and those around you very, very prosperous!

Celebrate Your Life Purpose with Others Through Service

Helping Others Through Public Service

Many people feel the need and desire to help others. A good way to do this is through public service. Public service can be helping others in a myriad of different ways. By serving the public, you may be working with people directly in a one-on-one manner, in groups or helping humankind in its entirety. Doing "one-on-one" service you may be mentoring a young person about a future choice. In a group it might be by working with senior citizens to teach them how to use computers for the first time. A scientist may be helping mankind by developing a vaccine that cures people of an illness. The scientists may never see the people they are helping however their work is a public service nonetheless.

By Helping Others, You are Helping Yourself

By helping others, you are in turn helping yourself. There are many benefits of helping others, some benefits are visible while others may not be however are just as important. By helping others, you are growing your "sphere of influence" meeting new people, establishing contacts, which from a business point-of-view, may lead to more financial prosperity coming your way. On an emotional level, helping others brings tremendous personal satisfaction. You, yes *you*, make a difference in someone else's life. Your selfless acts could well be positively changing the course of someone else's life by improving people lives, making their lives better, and making it worth living. By doing your "work", by helping others, you will help people find their "work". There is no greater gift to give to others than the gift of doing one's "work" while we are here on this planet and for you to be the person who showed them to use their own special gifts.

How do I Go About Helping Others?

Helping others does not have to be an elaborate production. It can be as simple as going to your local hospital, religious group, town hall and asking the question, "How can I help?" All helping is honorable and worthy. You may want to make an assessment of your skills and help others with your specific skills. For example, if you know how to set up computers you may want to donate your time to a local charity and set up their computer system. If you are blessed with financial prosperity you may want to make a donation to a worthy cause or organization. There are so many different ways you can help others and be of service. You choose the method that is right for you and watch your life change for the better; see the prosperity start flowing!

You are truly prosperous when you help others. As you help others you are sharing your prosperity. When you share your prosperity, it will come back to you many, many times over!

Below are some resources where you can be of service in helping others. This list is by no means complete and can be used as a starting point for your search:

1. **Volunteer Match**

   www.VolunteerMatch.org

2. **ServiceLeader.org**

   www.ServiceLeader.org/new/virtual/

3. **Extra Hands for ALS**

   www.ExtraHands.org/

4. **Charity Focus**

   my.CharityFocus.org/login/

5. **Network for Good**

   www.NetworkForGood.org/

6. **Big Brothers Big Sisters**

   www.bbbsa.org/

7. **Red Cross**

   http://www.RedCross.org/

8. **Angel Wish – Help Children Living With HIV-AIDS**

   www.AngelWish.org/

EXERCISE:

In the exercise below, make a listing of your skills then think about who might be able to use them or benefit from them.

My Skills in Helping Others

1. _____
2. _____
3. _____
4. _____
5. _____
6. _____

Who Needs My Skills

1. _____
2. _____
3. _____
4. _____
5. _____
6. _____

Help Others with their Life Purpose

I'm sure you will be meeting others that will be naturally attracted to you for living your life purpose and doing your true work. You will be radiant and those around you will be taking notice of how you feel and look full of joy and happiness. You may want to give them guidance so they can achieve their life purpose.

What a wonderful world this would be if we all lived our true life purpose, helping others and helping ourselves to be the best people we can be.

How such a world would benefit all of humankind and future generations.

NOTES

NOTES

Chapter 4: Strategic Business Planning: The Power of Planning Your Work and Working Your Plan

"Every minute you spend in planning saves 10 minutes in execution; this gives you a 1,000 percent Return on Energy!" – Brian Tracy

The Business Plan

In starting your own business or any major new venture it makes good sense to get a clear understanding as to what you are getting yourself into, financially and otherwise. The business plan is the tool to help and guide you as to how to get started in setting up and running a business. A business plan is a document that summarizes the operational and financial objectives of a business and contains the detailed plans and budgets showing how the objectives are to be realized. Because the business plan contains detailed financial projections, forecasts about your business's performance, and a strategic marketing and plan, it's an incredibly useful tool for business planning and usually required if you need to get any type of financing.

The purpose of this book is to guide you how to set up and run a business, there are two examples of business plans so you can get a better understanding of setting up and running your own business. The first example is a business plan for a service related business and the second business plan is for a product related business. Sample business plans are from the **www.MyOwnBusiness.org** website.

I would like to remind you of the following which is in the Publisher's Note at the beginning of the book. In your journey to operating a successful business. This book is designed to provide accurate and authoritative information in regard to the subject matter covered. When addressing financial matters in this manual and any of our websites, videos, newsletters or other content, the author has taken every effort to ensure he accurately represent his programs and their ability to improve your life or grow your business. However, there is no guarantee that you will get any results or earn any money using any of his ideas, tools, strategies or recommendations, and we do not purport any "get rich schemes" on any of our websites. Nothing on our websites is a promise or guarantee of earnings. Your level of success in attaining similar results is dependent upon a number of factors, including your skill, knowledge, ability, dedication, business savvy, network, and financial situation, to name a few. Because these factors differ according to individuals, we cannot and do not guarantee your success, income level, or ability to earn revenue. You alone are responsible for your actions and results in life and business. Any forward-looking statements outlined on our websites are simply my opinion and thus are not guarantees or promises of actual performance. It should be clear to you that by law I make no guarantees that you will achieve any results from our ideas or models presented on our websites, and we offer no professional legal, medical, psychological or financial advice. It is sold with the understanding that neither the author nor the publisher is engaged in rendering legal, accounting or other professional service. If legal advice or other expert assistance is required, the services of a professional person should be sought.

Sample Business Plan

(Service Business Plan))

SMITH E-COMMERCE CONSULTING

MARY SMITH

Last Update: August 22, 2016

SECTION 1: THE BUSINESS PROFILE

Description of My Business

I plan to provide a complete service for the design, installation and maintenance of E-commerce marketing functions for my retail clients. I intend to evaluate the success of each installation and follow up to make changes to improve the effectiveness of the each site.

Targeted Market and Customers

My customers will be small businesses that can enhance their present sales by the utilization of E-commerce. Typical clients will require sites for the dual purpose of providing 24-hour information to customers as well as providing a purchasing venue. Potential clients are businesses in which E-commerce can provide additional incremental sales. The businesses will range widely: from restaurants to neighborhood drugstores.

Growth Trends In This Business

The market for my services is growing at an unprecedented rate. In 2004 and 2005, year-end holiday shopping increased 25% each year.

Can you document from trade sources the anticipated rate of growth of your industry? If industry sources are not available, you will need to give a logical explanation as to the trend and potential of your intended market. This segment will provide you and your backers with information as to whether your market is growing or shrinking.

Pricing Power

Initially, my pricing power will be limited by what other consultants charge for their time. However, I expect my business to be built by favorable word-of-mouth and my services to command a somewhat higher schedule of rates than average. I therefore expect that my reputation will gain me a degree of pricing power. Another factor is if my type of services are rendered ineffectively, it can be very costly and of no value to a client. On the other hand, if done well (by myself) the services can be affordable and immensely valuable. By gaining this reputation, I expect to be well paid for my work.

SECTION 2: THE VISION AND THE PEOPLE

Through my work experience and my former moonlight business, I possess unique skills to provide specialized E-commerce services. Also, I have had a long-term desire to be in business full time for myself and to utilize this knowledge. I have worked with many hardware and software vendors and Web site designers. Utilizing the resources of these associates, I can demonstrate competency in all aspects of successful E-commerce implementation. I am passionately committed to my new business and have the realism to make inevitable hard choices.

Educational Credentials

My education includes: _____grade school, graduation from _____high school (class of _____).

My higher education includes a _____degree earned in _____ at_____ university, _____ year.

In _____school I participated in the following activities   (student council, student body officer, sorority/fraternity, clubs, etc.) I have also taken the following courses and seminars: My Own Business Internet Course, _____, _____.

My hobbies are: _____

My ongoing education includes subscriptions to the following professional journals: Wall Street Journal, Plastics World, etc.

I belong to the following professional and service organizations: National Association of Importers, Rotary Club, etc.

Work Experience Related to My Intended Business

My work experience has been as follows:

1995 – 1998: Position_____ at _____Co. Describe your work
                responsibilities in detail:
_____
1998 – 2009 Position _____at _____Co. Describe your work
                responsibilities in detail:
_____

SECTION 2: THE VISION AND THE PEOPLE

My work experience with _____company mentioned above included responsibility for Web-site design, implementation and maintenance. I have included a list of work references and character references in Exhibit A, attached.

I belong to the following professional organizations: National Association of E-commerce Designers

My consulting service will require specialized knowledge in all aspects of implementing E-commerce sites for small businesses. I have been moonlighting in this activity for 2 years and have successfully executed contracts with 5 small businesses. (See Exhibit __ including references, attached). I feel that this background qualifies me to undertake this business on a full time basis.

SECTION 3: COMMUNICATIONS

Computer and Communications Tools

My business equipment requirements consist primarily of computer and communications tools. I have all of the following resources in place:

Resource Requirements:

Communications
Enter a description of all communications equipment.

Telephones
Enter a description of all telephone equipment.

Facsimile
Enter a description of all fax equipment.

Computers
Enter a description of all computer equipment.

Internet
Enter a description of necessary Internet providers.

SECTION 4: BUSINESS ORGANIZATION

Business Organization

The form of business organization:

Initially I will be starting up the operation of Smith E-Commerce Consulting as a proprietorship. At my business grows and at a time my attorney feels appropriate, I will begin operating as a Limited Liability Corporation.

My main focus will be on the creation of websites that are user and search engine friendly for on-line purchasing functions.

SECTION 5: LICENSES PERMITS AND BUSINESS NAMES

Due Diligence Procedures for Licenses, Permits and Business Name

DBA: Smith E-Commerce Consulting. My intellectual property lawyer, an important consultant since I will be creating intellectual property for my clients, will do a search and if possible register my DBA (Doing Business As) name and logo.

Zoning: My start-up will be as a home based business. I have been advised by the City Hall clerk's office that I will qualify as an approved home business. My future office premises will be in a commercially zoned office space.

Licenses: The licenses I will need at the local, state, and federal level include:

Local: Municipal Business License from City Hall.

State: A state identification number will be secured from the Board of Equalization.

Federal: A federal EIN number will be secured from the IRS

Trademark: My trademarks will include my logo (to be designed) and my DBA name.

Sellers Permit: While I will not be charging sales tax on my services, at a future time when I begin marketing Internet equipment, I will secure a sellers resale permit from the state board of equalization.

SECTION 6: INSURANCE

I plan to consult with insurance agent Dan Deductable, who has been recommended by my accountant. My insurance coverage will be maintained in a "package" type insurance policy tailored for small service business such as mine.

SECTION 7: LOCATION AND LEASING

The criteria for my future office space will include:

- Space requirements including growth
- Site analysis study if needed (attach)
- Demographic study if needed (attach)
- Lease check-off list (attach)
- Estimated occupancy cost as a % of sales
- Zoning and use approvals

SECTION 8: ACCOUNTING AND CASH FLOW

Accounting

Attached as a separate exhibit is my starting balance sheet and projected income statements for the first six months to one year.

Cash Flow Planning

Attached is an exhibit of my first year's cash flow projecting including estimated sales, all costs and capital investments.

Following is a checklist of all expense items included in the cash flow projection.

Analysis of Costs

Since my service business will initially be essentially intellectual property and advice, my start-up costs will be based on my living expenses and costs related to the set-up of websites, maintenance and operation of my office equipment, communication and computer functions. However, pricing will include overhead, general and administrative expenses as if I were operating out of leased premises.

Internal Controls

As a service provider, I will personally be the only person controlling expenses, accounting and check signing. But at no time in the future will I delegate the authority for large purchase orders or check signing.

SECTION 9: HOW I WILL FINANCE THE BUSINESS

Financing Strategy

Attached is a spreadsheet showing all of the sources of my start-up capital. The major part of my start-up costs will come from savings. I have saved some money every month since I was fifteen years old and this nest egg will be my major source of initial working capital and equipment. I have also maintained three credit cards with balances paid promptly each month. The use of these credit lines will be for reserve purposes only and provided there are sources of repayment for any use of the cards. For example, to tide me over during periods of outstanding receivables. Once I have three years of profitable earnings statements, I plan to seek a regular line of bank credit. At a future time when I will begin marketing Internet technology hardware and software along with my services, I will look to my vendors for credit and advertising assistance.

SECTION 10: E-COMMERCE

E-Commerce Plans

Since my business will be to deliver E-Commerce solutions to retail businesses, it will be important for my clients to have outstanding website functions, furnishing valuable information and user-friendly navigation. Marketing by work-of-mouth referrals will be initially the most single means of new business. Once my initial client's sites are live and successful, I plan to start making calls on larger clients, using my successful installations as references.

As the backlog builds, I plan to build a team of outsourced vendors, including programmers, website designers, search engine consultants and copy experts. Ultimately, Smith Consulting will become a turnkey outsourced E-commerce department for major retail operators.

E-Commerce Budgeting

My initial costs will be living expenses, purchase of additional office supplies, computer equipment and communications devices which are outlined as follows:

E-Commerce Competition

My best competitors are individual I.T. experts who moonlight as website developers and individuals who practice full-time. I plan to project a full-time business-like entity that merchants can look to as an ongoing and primary resource for designing, installing and continually upgrading their Internet marketing of goods and services. By emphasizing my full-time commitment as a consulting professional, I intend to grow to ongoing contracts with major players of retail Internet marketing.

SECTION 11: BUYING A BUSINESS OR FRANCHISE

Looking into the future, I may find opportunities to grow by purchasing the consulting practices of other Website designers. For example, to become a national firm there may be designers in other major markets who have reasons to sell their businesses and whose acquisition could result in "Smith Consulting Group" becoming a major national resource for major chain retailers.

Before starting my practice at home, I will have my consulting team in place, including business lawyer, accountant and intellectual property lawyer.

Acquisition of other businesses in my field will require a formal due-diligence checklist to investigate all aspects of the purchase:

Sellers' records to be inspected: Financial statements, income tax returns, sales backlog, cash deposit records, utility bills, accounts payable and receivable, backlog, financial comparisons of similar businesses, etc.

Inspections and approval of leases and contracts.

Appraisals, as appropriate.

If a franchise, interview with randomly selected franchisees.

Finance plan for acquisitions: includes sources such as seller financing.

Market conditions.

Value of goodwill.

Method of purchase: stock, assets, etc.

SECTION 12: MARKETING

Marketing Plan

My initial marketing will be to spend four hours per day on sales calls to local merchants who are not engaged in E-commerce. I will take initial assignments at reduced fees in order to establish a growing portfolio of successful users. I feel that the time spend on personal calls will outperform other means of marketing. Also, I plan to promote and conduct free seminars that are addressed to local business owners. From these seminars I would make follow-up calls to seek out clients. I may collaborate with my C.P.A. in the conduct of these seminars.

Advertising and Promotion Plans

My initial advertising budget will be limited to expenses connected with seminars including room expense, local newspaper advertising and other expenses connected with seminar programming.

Purchasing and Inventory Control

Since I will be dealing entirely with intellectual property, my expenses connected with inventory and problems associated with purchasing goods will be eliminated.

SECTION 12: MARKETING

The Competition

As covered in Section 10 of this plan, my principal competitors will be either moonlight operators or established firms.

How I Plan to Take Advantage of Competitors Weak Points

My emphasis will be to remove myself from competition by furnishing ongoing marketing advice, equipment upgrades, and new market opportunities to clients. The goal will be to establish, in effect, an ongoing consulting service to my clients to keep them on the cutting edge of not only technology but in e-commerce marketing techniques. I will be collaborating with my team of advisors including C.P.A. and attorney to be furnishing ongoing business insights as well as pitfalls to avoid.

Section 13: Growth Program

Expansion

My objectives of growth will be to expand from local individual businesses to small chains and ultimately to the major e-commerce chains throughout the country. It will be important to stay focused on providing all aspects of E-commerce solutions but not become engaged in unrelated IT responsibilities. By keeping my focus on E-commerce, I can carve out a niche that over time can become a huge consultancy while avoiding competing with the major players in the IT hardware and software fields.

Handling Major Problems

An important part of my planning includes how I plan to handle adverse business conditions. The greatest risk I face is a large drop off in sales which would impact future liquidity. Attached are two pro-forma (estimated) cash flows, one with a 25% reduction in forecasted sales and another with a 40% drop in sales. In each case it will require prompt reduction in costs to avoid loss of liquidity (running out of money). In this manner I will have a plan in place to handle future cyclical swings in my business. These two cash flows are attached as exhibits.

SECTION 14: INTERNATIONAL TRADE

Due   Diligence   Procedures   for   International   Trade

Export Counseling: I do not plan to operate out of my own country for the next five to ten years. But at some point I anticipate that Smith Consulting will be engaged by multinational firms that will require me to have specialized knowledge of international business. My first step at this point will be to retain legal counsel specializing in international transactions. My international trade advisor will need to assist me in outlining the following preparations.

Export Readiness: Describe the economic reasons and justification for my plans. Outline the personnel, budget and procedures I plan to implement.

Agent/distributor Agreement: Provide a draft of your agent/distributor agreement and the agents/distributors I am considering doing business with.

Analysis of Competitive Considerations: Explain the due diligence resources to be used in the evaluation opportunities including appropriateness of your business.

Evaluation of Country Risk: Explain the resources to be used in the evaluation of the country risk (is the country in good standing?) including potential sources of financing.

Describe your plans to insure protection of intellectual property rights.

Describe marketing and advertising plans.

Evaluate potential problems regarding product adaptation to standards and measurements.

Describe the licensing requirements for the export of your services.

I plan to use a payroll service provider from the initial start-up, even including the early times I will be working by myself. This cost can be delegated for less than it would cost me to be handling start-up payroll, payroll deductions, local state and federal withholdings. I have received three proposals and intend to use _____company.

Before hiring my first employee or delegating services to outsourced suppliers, I will prepare job descriptions for each responsibility.

I have attached a copy of the job application I plan to use which is a standard form available at my office supplier.

When I begin to hire employees, I strongly feel that there will need to be an ample package of benefits for my employees in order to avoid turnover due to larger firms having more generous plans. My plan will include paid vacations, full medical coverage for my employees (not their dependents) and the company contributing $_____ per year to a Simple IRA plan.

I plan to complete an employee handbook before hiring any employees.

SECTION 15: MANAGING EMPLOYEES

My initial and ongoing training programs for employees are attached as an exhibit.

Since future payroll problems can include great legal risks, at the time of hiring the first employee I plan to retain an attorney whose practice is limited to labor law.

SECTION 16: HOME BASED BUSINESS ISSUES

1. Factors in Starting as a home based business:

   1. My previous experience qualifies for conducting my own consulting business.
   2. For me, a home based start is appropriate and will keep my costs down.
   3. I can fully utilize the Internet and communications tools at home.
   4. My home based zoning and licensing have been approved.
   5. As a full-time home based business I can project a professional image as my bigger competitors.

2. The Home Based Business Format

   At the very beginning I plan to start as a moonlighter (without quitting my job) then switch to full time business at home, and later in an office setting.

   Make preparations before quitting my job.

3. Conflict of interest management

   Since I will initially be starting a business at home while working at my present job, I plan to strictly avoid conflict-of-interest risks by compartmentalizing my business completely away from my job responsibilities.

4. Operating personnel

   I do not plan to use any other family members in the home based operation of Smith Consulting, except for help in marketing seminars. My high school son, however, is fascinated with the prospects of a family business and is hoping to learn the basics as I expand.

NOTES

Sample Business Plan
(Product Business Plan)

WIDGET CORPORATION

JAMES JONES

Last Update: August 22, 2016

SECTION 1: THE BUSINESS PROFILE

Description of My Business

I plan to market a complete line of bathroom accessories including "squeezies", soap dishes, toothbrush holders, coat hooks, and towel bars. The product line will be designed in my home office and manufactured and packaged in China.

Targeted Market and Customers

My customers will be discount department store chains with good credit ratings and reputations for prompt-payment. These will include Albertson's, Costco, Fleming, Wal-Mart, K-Mart, Target, and selected others.

Growth Trends In This Business

The market for household bathroom accessories is growing as the population grows and new household formations take place. This is especially true in expanding economies as the standards of living make further gains. Also household purchases are increasingly being made through large chain discount retailers which I plan to focus on serving.

Pricing Power

I will not initially enjoy pricing power in marketing Widget accessories. Discount chains will be primarily interested in price. In order to achieve lower costs than my larger competitors I plan to do the following: _____.

My ultimate goal is to build a line so unique and promote it so effectively that consumers will be willing to pay a premium. My long-term objective is to build a market that is not entirely based on price. My unique features will include: _____.

The Vision

I have a long-term plan to be in business for myself and to utilize the specialized business knowledge I have gained. The business relationships I have developed include vendors, discount chain buyers and manufacturing resources. They are:
_____,
_____, _____. (List and explain in detail how they will help you).

The reasons that I feel my plans are realistic are: _____. I am the right person to pursue this opportunity because: _____.

There are special market conditions that are favorable to my getting started at this time.
They are: _____.

The People

Work Experience Related To My intended Business

My work experience has been as follows:
1995 – 1998 Position_____ at _____Co. Describe your work
responsibilities in detail:
_____

1998 – 2006 Product Manager at ABC Imports Co. Describe your work
responsibilities in detail:
_____

I have included a list of work references and character references as Exhibit A

I have personal contacts in Hong Kong and Singapore who are ready to assist in the design, production, and packaging of the WIDGET line. Two large discount chains have encouraged me to make presentations to them.

SECTION 2: THE VISION AND THE PEOPLE

Personal Background and Education Credentials

EDUCATION CREDENTIALS:

My education includes: _____ grade school, graduation from _____ high school (class of ____).

My higher education includes a _____ degree earned in _____ at_____, _____ year.

In _____ school I participated in the following activities   (student council, student body officer, sorority/fraternity, clubs, etc.) I have also taken the following courses and seminars: My Own Business Internet Course, _____, and _____.

My hobbies are: _____

My ongoing education includes subscriptions to the following professional journals: Wall Street Journal, Plastics World, Fortune Magazine, Business Week.

I belong to the following professional and service organizations: National Association of Importers, American Plastics Association, The International Chamber of Commerce.

Computer and Communications Tools

I plan to take advantage of all the computer and communications tools presently available to establish myself on the same level playing field as my large competitors. Following are the tentative specifications and budget for this equipment.

Resource Requirements:

Communications:
Enter a description of all communications equipment.

Enter a budget for all communications equipment.

Telephones:
Enter a description of all telephone equipment.

Enter a budget for all telephone equipment.

Facsimile:
Enter a description of all fax equipment.

Enter a budget for all fax equipment.

Computers:
Enter a description of all computer equipment.

Enter a budget for all computer equipment.

Internet:
Enter a description of necessary Internet providers.

Enter a budget for Internet access.

SECTION 4: ORGANIZATION

Business Organization

I plan to form a corporation for my business. It is my intention to grow Widget into a large firm with international relationships. The initial and ongoing costs of operating as a corporation will be a necessary business expense. Also, since a properly run corporation will afford me some limits of liability, I feel this is the right form of business for me. I intend to depend on my attorney to handle all aspects of setting up the corporation and maintaining proper corporate records.

Professional Consultants

I feel it is important that my team of professional advisors be in place before I start in business. Here is a list of these professionals:

Attorney: Suzie Catchum
Accountant: Norman Numbers
Insurance Agent: Paul Premium
Banker: Douglas Deeppockets
E-commerce Consultant: Mary Smith
Other: _____
Other: _____

SECTION 5: BUSINESS LICENSES AND PERMITS

My due-diligence procedures for licenses, permits and business names will be as follows:

DBA: I plan to do business as Premier Widget Corporation.

Zoning: Initially I will be working out of my home.   When a staff is required I plan to move to a C-1 office space with a short-term lease with options to extend and expand.

Licenses: Licenses will be secured from appropriate authorities:

Local permits: Working at home: City Clerk at City Hall

State licensing: An account will be set up with the State Board of Equalization for sales tax reporting.

Federal: No federal licensing will be required.

Trademark: My attorney is conducting a trademark search for Premier Widget Corporation. If available, we will follow our attorney's instructions in protecting the name.

EIN: An Employer Identification Number has been secured from the IRS.

Sellers Permit: None are required at the present time.

SECTION 6: INSURANCE

I plan to use the services of Paul Premium, my insurance agent. My insurance policies and limits of coverage are as follows:

Mr. Premium will provide me with a tabulation of all policies and limits of liability.

The company will not be self-insurance on any insurable risks.

Worker's Compensation insurance will be available from State Fund Insurance when I hire the first employee.

SECTION 7: LOCATION AND LEASING

During my start-up phase of approximately 6-12 months, I plan to operate out of my home office. Once my business is established, my initial office requirement will be approximately 1,000 square feet with two private offices and a secretarial area. My office criteria will include:

1. Convenience to my home.
2. A short-term lease of 1 - 2 years with two 1-year options.
3. A lease provision that the landlord provides me expansion space as required with a "kick-out" clause if expansion space is not available.
4. Office layout including tenant improvements provided by the landlord. See Exhibit "C".
5. Lawyer review of the lease.
6. Use of the Lease Check-off list that is attached as an exhibit.

The use of these location criteria will gain me experience in handling much larger leases for space in the relatively near future. Future growth plans include warehousing of merchandise. I will be incurring large lease obligations that will be carefully reviewed.

Location Criteria
- Space requirements
- Future requirements
- Site analysis study (when needed)
- Demographic study (when needed)
- Lease check-off list (when needed)
- Estimated occupancy cost as a % of sales
- Zoning and use approvals

SECTION 8: ACCOUNTING AND CASH FLOW

Accounting

My knowledge of accounting is: _____. (*If you are deficient in basic accounting knowledge, then state how you intend to gain this needed know-how.*)

My accountant: I plan to work with C.P.A. Norman Numbers.

Accounting and payroll software programs: I will be using the following systems: _____.

Method of accounting: I will use the accrual method of accounting since this is generally required by the Internal Revenue Service for businesses dealing with manufacturing and inventory.

Business records: I will keep Widget accounts and records separate from my personal records.

Tax issues: My accountant, Mr. Numbers, will help me set up records for payments of social security tax, estimated income tax payments, payroll taxes and state withholding and sales taxes. My federal employer identification number (FEIN) is: _____.   My state identification number is: _____.

Quarterly returns: Taxes will be paid in the appropriate time frames. Mr. Numbers will help me set up resale permit records for reporting to my state franchise tax board.

Bank account reconciliation: Bank accounts will be reconciled on a monthly basis.

Balance sheet: Attached is a separate exhibit of my starting balance sheet. Included is a schedule of equipment and fixtures needed that will appear on my balance sheet.

Income statements: Attached are my projected income statements for the first six months and one year.

SECTION 8: ACCOUNTING AND CASH FLOW

Internal Controls

My accountant, Norman Numbers, is experienced in my type of business, which includes international trade. He will help me set up a system of internal controls to make sure that Widget Corporation will receive all of its income without any of it being siphoned off by waste, fraud, dishonest employees or carelessness.

This will include an inventory policy, including who can sign for goods and services and who controls the release of goods and services out the door. Included in the internal control policy will be the requirement that the only person authorized to sign purchase orders, make capital acquisitions and sign checks will be myself personally.

Cash Flow Planning

Attached is an exhibit of my one-year cash flow analysis, including estimated sales, all costs and capital requirements. I have included a checklist of all expense items for input into my cash flow projections.

Analysis of Costs

Attached is an itemized cost-breakdown of each individual Widget product that will be in my initial line. My initial target mark-up will be _____%.

SECTION 9: FINANCING

Financing Strategy

My requirements for start-up capital are as follows:

Attached is a list of expenses for which I will require either start-up capital or financing. These items include buying supplies, getting a computer, equipment and fixtures, tooling, travel expenses and start-up overhead expenses. These expenses are included in my monthly cash flow projection to indicate the ongoing requirements for cash.

My sources of financing for starting my business are indicated in the following spreadsheet. While I will not be depending on banks for financing, there will be other resources available to me such as leasing of equipment and fixtures, credit from suppliers, mortgage financing, etc. My referrals include the following helpful contacts to lending institutions: my accountant, the Small Business Administration, friends, relatives, etc.

I am prepared to make presentations to potential lenders. My presentation kit includes this business plan, my personal financial statement and personal tax returns. I will be prepared to be specific in my needs for financing, the payback program and my sources of repayment. I will furnish potential lenders a cash flow projection showing sources of repayments and I will be conservative in my forecasts. A portfolio of referrals will be prepared for the finance package.

E-Commerce Plans

A website focusing on business-to-business E-commerce will be an important tool in my overall marketing program. I plan to build and install the www.widgetcorp.com website, which I have already registered. This will permit my discount department store customers to have access to my product line and to order (and reorder) merchandise via this website. I plan to hire Mary Smith of Smith E-Commerce Consulting Company to design, install and maintain this site.

The features of the www.widgetcorp.com site will include:

- It will be easy to use with good navigational features and prompt loading.
- The site will provide useful content including detailed information about all items in my product line.
- Purchasing procedures on a B-to-B basis will be designed and implemented.
- I intend to use the site to generate client feedback to help improve every aspect of my product line, operation and business procedures.

E-Commerce   Budgeting

The cost breakdown of implementing my e-commerce activities are as follows:

E-Commerce Competition

The use of business-to-business e-commerce has become standard in my industry and is an important marketing tool. It is my intention to maintain a website that will project the image of a fresh and dynamic resource to my customers. I plan to keep abreast of the website developments of my competitors and to constantly improve my site.

My best competitors utilize e-commerce as follows (provide details). My strategy to improve on these practices include: describe.

SECTION 11: BUSINESS ACQUISITIONS STRATEGY

Due Diligence Procedures for Acquisitions

I may have opportunities to acquire businesses in the future. In order to position myself to investigate acquisitions intelligently, the following "due diligence" process will be adhered to.

I will use a team of experts to give specific advice on the various components of the acquisition:
- Attorney
- Accountant
- Banker
- Broker
- Equipment supplier
- Other business owners

The following information will be required:
1. Sellers records and verification of revenues
2. Current financial statements
3. Cash deposit records
4. Supplier bills
5. Financial comparisons of similar businesses
6. Other _____

Valuation analysis will include:

- Basis for valuation: appraisals, etc.
- Method of purchase: stock, assets, etc.
- If a franchise, interview with randomly selected franchisees
- Evaluation of predictable future earnings
- Status of seller's motivation to sell
- Sources of acquisition financing
- Inspection of seller's personal and business tax returns
- Evaluation of leases and contracts
- Quality of improvements
- Quality and size of inventory. Obsolete merchandise?
- Condition of receivables
- Status of payables
- Status of verified order backlog
- Evaluation of customer relationships and goodwill
- Evaluate government approvals and licenses
- Status of pending litigation
- Other _____

SECTION 12: MARKETING

Marketing Plan

I plan to focus all initial marketing efforts on establishing a beachhead at one large discount department store chain. I will personally be responsible for the contacts with the appropriate buyers. My complete line will be presented as a package including display accessories that tie into the merchandising policies of each chain. Initially my price structure will be based on a maximum markup of _____% in order to provide a strong price incentive. I will be depending on the combination of fresh styling, quality and price to break into this market.

Advertising and Promotion Plans

Short Range Plan (6 to 12 months): Initially my advertising and promotion will be done on an entirely personal basis without any budget for paid advertising. My customers require personal visitation by the CEO's of their vendors. It will be my plan to limit my advertising budget to personal travel expenses in making these presentations and follow-up presentations.

Mid-Range Plan (12 – 36 months): To establish brand recognition at the retail level, I plan to budget _____% of my sales to joint advertising with my discount department store customers. I will solicit presentations from local advertising agencies.

Long Range Plan: I plan to aggressively build brand recognition and loyalty by budgeting _____% of sales, which will be allocated between space advertising in trade journals, appropriate consumer magazines and joint advertising with my customers.

Purchasing and Inventory Control

For replenishment of stocks I plan to participate in just-in-time tracking with my customers, utilizing their on-line business-to-business computer systems in place. As much as possible, warehousing will be kept to a minimum by use of direct and rapid delivery systems.

The following procedures will be implemented:

We will ask for 30-day payment terms and offer 2% discount for 10 days.
An inventory control system will be maintained.
All merchandise received will be counted and inspected.
We will pay our contractors on time and be loyal to them.
We will ask for and take term discounts.
Purchase Orders will include:
    Price and terms
    Price protection
Always in writing:
    Complete specifications
    Delivery deadlines
    All promises will be verified in writing
    Appropriate contingencies will be included in purchase orders
    Any changes or extras must have prior approval in writing

Internal controls will be in place for shipping and receiving

The Competition

My principal competitor is Colossal Plastics Company. I have included a list of all major competitors in this business and a brief sketch including to whom they sell. (Provide a tabulation of these competitors).

SECTION 12: MARKETING

How I Plan to Take Advantage of my Competitors Weak Points

My biggest competitor is Colossal Plastics Company, which has a 20-year history of success and has gained strong brand-recognition. But they have developed a large overhead structure, which I will not have. They are also slow to make changes and upgrades to their line of products. I plan to overcome their leadership with fresh new designs, artwork and attractive packaging and to be priced very competitively. I intend to continually introduce additions and refinements to the line.

Also, my end-user profile is for younger families who are not impressed by old-line brand names. Operating with a very low overhead, I believe I can gain a foothold in this market. A similar profile of my other principal competitors is enclosed indicating their weak spots and how I plan to capitalize on these deficiencies.

SECTION 13: GROWTH PROGRAM

Expansion Plans

Once my business has been established I plan to implement the following growth strategy. I anticipate it will take approximately _____(months or years) to gain sufficient experience and level of profits before any expansion plans are implemented.

My growth strategy will be guided by the following:

I will not set an inflexible timetable for expansion but will wait until a sound basis of experience, earnings and cash flow is achieved. (If you intend to expand as a chain of stores or units, here's where you should take a stand to say that your initial pilot operation will be on a sound earnings basis before you begin to add more units.)

Accounting and cash flow controls will be in place with profit and loss statements prepared for individual expansion units on a _____(monthly, etc) basis.

Internal controls for accounting, money handling and inventory will be in place.

My attorney will review all documentation regarding expansion. This will include leases, employment and incentive agreements, licensing and franchise agreements, important commitments with vendors and customers, etc.

It is my intention that expansion plans will not change my policy of taking adequate time for my family.

Hiring and training policies will be in place. Fringe benefit plans will be in place.

My intention is to delegate authority and responsibility to expansion management personnel with the following conditions in place:

1. Managers will be motivated by a profit incentive plan that will be tied to manager's individual success. My plan will be in writing, simply stated and will call for frequent periods of accountability. A sample of my manager's incentive compensation plan is attached.

2. Capital allocations and signing checks will not be delegated.

3. I intend to maintain an ongoing study of my competitors. Their successes and failures will help me form guidelines on what to do and not to do.

I plan to development profitable pilot operations before undertaking full-scale production. Analysis will be made of sources of financing, cash flow, accounting systems, incentive compensation plans for managers, and economics of scale.

Handling Major Problems

My policy in handling problems will be to identify and acknowledge problems promptly and honestly. I plan to put the following policies into effect promptly if the following adverse scenarios emerge during my growth program:

The risk of running out of cash: I plan to maintain very frequent (_____monthly?) cash flow projections. Forecasts for income, expenses and unanticipated contingencies will be stated conservatively. Any periods of cash deficits will be remedied promptly by cutting costs to maintain a positive cash flow and profitability.

A drop in sales or insufficient sales:

1. I will be prepared to take prompt remedial steps by cutting costs.
2. I will improve every aspect of product value, performance and image
3. I will seek out new ways to expand sales by _____.
4. I plan to stick with this specialized business that I know best unless fatally defective.

Dishonesty, theft, and shrinkage: I intend to implement the same policies that have been proven by _____ company, one of my biggest competitors.

Business recessions: I am prepared to promptly cut costs to maintain liquidity. I will also be on the lookout for good business opportunities during periods of adversity. Scenarios of adverse conditions will be prepared and solutions on how I intend to respond to them included. Included in this analysis will be projected cash flow projections based on a 25% and 45% reduction in sales. The main objective will be to promptly initiate cost reductions in order to preserve ongoing liquidity.

SECTION 14: INTERNATIONAL TRADE

Due   Diligence   Procedures   for   International   Trade

Export Counseling: My team of counselors will include a consultant or lawyer who specializes in international trade. All documentation will be approved by this consultant.

Export Readiness: International trade will become a key part of my success because of the dependency on importing my precision molded products. This dependence is based on the cost advantages of imported goods. Initially, I will personally be responsible for all transactions.

Agent/distributor Agreement: A draft of my agent/distributor agreement (prepared by; my consultant) and the agents/distributors I am considering to do business with is attached.

Analysis of Competitive Considerations: I will retain my consultant to initially perform the due diligence in evaluating opportunities.

Evaluation of Country Risk: I will participate in the study of resources to be evaluated and potential country risk, including potential sources of financing.

Protection of intellectual property rights: My intellectual property lawyer will be responsible for handling intellectual property diligence in the protection of my names, products and trade secrets.

Marketing: My marketing and advertising plans will emphasize the low price/high value nature of Widget products for sale through large discount retailers.

Standards and measurements: Potential problems regarding product adaptation to standards and measurements will be vetted and resolved where necessary.

Licenses: Our international consultant will determine all licensing requirements for export and/or import of our products. I plan to market Widget products throughout the world.

SECTION 15: MANAGING EMPLOYEES

Training Policies

Initially I will personally handle sales to my discount department store customers. As my business expands, I intend to begin marketing to smaller retailers. I will hire sales associates who can gain the confidence of smaller buyers who want to deal with vendors that are knowledgeable and helpful. To achieve these qualities I will look for the following characteristics in marketing employees. People who:

- Like what they do
- Are quick learners
- Project a pleasant and positive image
- Like people and relate well to them
- Are helpful to customers and fellow associates
- Are ambitious and seek to grow in responsibilities

I will follow a checklist in hiring marketing associates:

- Have a hiring policy in place, including written salary structure, commission compensation and perks
- Create job descriptions for everyone
- Conduct ongoing marketing meetings
- Have written policies and procedures on handling customer complaints
- Maintain clear guidelines for pricing policies and handling customer inquiries

I plan to outsource the handling of payroll and payroll accounting and reporting to the XYZ Services Company.

I have included copies of job descriptions for all employees I will be hiring during the first year.
Attached is a copy of the job application form and screening procedures I intend to use. Screening procedures will include drug testing, criminal records, checks with prior employers and proficiency at the job skills required.

Our benefits package will include 100% health coverage for employees but not for dependents. Three percent of annual wages will be contributed by the company towards employee's Simple IRA retirement plans. Vacation will be paid for up to two weeks per year.

Attached is a copy of my intended employee handbook.

Initial and ongoing training programs for employees will be mandatory and at company expense.

SECTION 15: MANAGING EMPLOYEES

Labor attorney, Mr. John Smith will be advising me on employee matters.

SECTION 16: HOME BASED BUSINESS

Factors in Selecting Home Based

1. I have had 15 years background in precision molded plastics plus marketing experience to chain store purchasing departments.

2. I will be starting Widget Corporation at home in order to conserve cash during the getting ready period.

3. The intensive use of Internet technology which I will deploy can be handled from my home base as well.

4. My home is zoned for a home based business such as the office requirements of Widget.

My Home Based Business Format
I will first start as a moonlighter, while keeping my regular job, and then when appropriate switch to full-time at home, and finally to operation out of suitable office quarters.

Conflict of Interest Management
During the initial period when I will be operating as a moonlighter (while still holding my job) I will observe all necessary measures to compartmentalize Widget away from my employment as well as avoidance of any conflict possibilities.

Operating Personnel While Operating from Home
During the home-based period of Widget, both my wife and our two high school sons will be acting in supportive roles: My wife handling accounting and website development and my sons helping with Internet researching of potential vendors.

Below is a **blank Business Plan** like the previous ones discussed. Feel free to use it to create your own business plan. Or you can use another Business Plan format that you like or even Business Plan software. The Business Plan will be required if you are seeking any type of funding especially from the government; be it federal, state or local; governments. It's also a good idea if you are seeking funding from private concerns or family as well.

The Business Plan is your blueprint of your business and the key to your success. The more you plan the less likely things can go wrong and when/if they do go wrong the quicker you can bounce back in the areas of time and money. Do not short cut this step. **It will give you clarity for your business and also makes you answer the tough questions that need to be answered in every business.**

NOTES

Blank Business Plan
(Product Business Plan)

YOUR COMPANY NAME HERE

YOUR NAME

Last Update: August 22, 2016

SECTION 1: THE BUSINESS PROFILE

Description of My Business

Targeted Market and Customers

Growth Trends In This Business

Pricing Power

SECTION 2: THE VISION AND THE PEOPLE

Educational Credentials

Work Experience Related to My Intended Business

SECTION 3: COMMUNICATIONS

Computer and Communications Tools

Resource Requirements:

Communications:

Enter a description of all communications equipment.

Telephones:

Enter a description of all telephone equipment.

Facsimile:

Enter a description of all fax equipment.

Computers:

Enter a description of all computer equipment.

Internet:

Enter a description of necessary Internet providers.

SECTION 4: BUSINESS ORGANIZATION

Business Organization

The form of business organization:

SECTION 5: LICENSES PERMITS AND BUSINESS NAMES

Due Diligence Procedures for Licenses, Permits and Business Name

DBA:

Zoning:

Licenses: The licenses I will need at the local, state, and federal level include:

Local:

State:

Federal:

Trademark:

Sellers Permit (Sales Tax Collection):

SECTION 6: INSURANCE

SECTION 7: LOCATION AND LEASING

SECTION 8: ACCOUNTING AND CASH FLOW

Accounting

Attached as a separate exhibit is my starting balance sheet and projected income statements for the first six months to one year.

Cash Flow Planning

Attached is an exhibit of my first year's cash flow projecting including estimated sales, all costs and capital investments.

Following is a checklist of all expense items included in the cash flow projection.

Analysis of Costs

Internal Controls

SECTION 9: HOW I WILL FINANCE THE BUSINESS

SECTION 10: E-COMMERCE

E-Commerce Plans

E-Commerce Budgeting

E-Commerce Competition

SECTION 11: BUYING A BUSINESS OR FRANCHISE

SECTION 12: MARKETING

Marketing Plan

Advertising and Promotion Plans

Purchasing and Inventory Control

SECTION 12: MARKETING

The Competition

How I Plan to Take Advantage of Competitors Weak Points

SECTION 13: GROWTH PROGRAM

Expansion

Handling Major Problems

SECTION 14: INTERNATIONAL TRADE

SECTION 16: HOME BASED BUSINESS ISSUES

NOTES

NOTES

Chapter 5: Marketing: You Go to the Marketplace - Even Better the Marketplace Comes to You!

5a. What is Marketing?

What is Marketing? The short answer is the action or business of promoting and selling products or services. Realistically, it's getting your products and/or services out into the market place in front of potential customers **AND/OR** having potential customer come to you (which is always more preferable ☺). **Marketing is interdependent (dependent on each other) with Selling.** Technically Selling is involved with the actual closing of deals Marketing is more concerned with getting in front of potential customers through various mediums like Advertising, Email Marketing and a host of other types of Marketing Strategies many mentioned below. Marketing usually works with Sales by providing the Sales people with **Leads** (people that have shown interest in your products/services). **Then the Sales person/people take the Leads and moves to convert them to closed deals.** If you are a "one-person company" then you are doing this yourself.

5b. Types of Marketing Strategies

Below are some Marketing Strategies that are currently in use in the marketplace. Which ones should you be using? It all depends on your **Target Market** (which I will be discussing shortly). It's best to get an understanding of what these Marketing Strategies are, how they work and their cost (in time and money to implement) then make decisions based on which Marketing Strategies that your Target Market use, that is, participate in on a regular basis.

1. **List Building – The Power is in the List!**

   The Prospect List, also known as "The List" is a very important part of your marketing efforts as it is the foundation of many of the preceding Marketing Strategies. How do you build your list? One way is through your website with an "opt in" box to your newsletter. Another method is when you go to business events and collect business cards. Yet another method is "joint ventures" with other like vendors. For example, you can offer a "Special Report" in exchange for the person's email address. As mentioned previously, this book is designed to give you the basics so your next step would be to learn about list building by reading books and learning from professional list builders. Just Google "List Building" and you will get a host of free and not free resources on how to build your list. The list can be Name and Address and/or just emails depending which you are going to use in your marketing efforts.

2. **Email Marketing**

   Once you have your list you can start email Marketing. Email marketing is directly marketing a commercial message to a group of people using email. In its broadest sense, every email sent to a potential or current customer could be considered email marketing. The most common type of email Marketing is the Newsletter. However, there are other types of email marketing strategies as well. The "Mini-Course", email with attachment (Document, Audio Clip, Video Clip) and other types as well which I'm sure will progress as the technology does.

3. **Internet Marketing**

    Using your website as a marketing tool. How do you do that? By placing your website address on: your business cards, brochures, on your voicemail message, when you speak with people, etc. You want to drive internet traffic to your website. Your website is your "Silent Sales Person" so it is to be designed in a manner to convert potential buyers into customers or at a minimum to contact you to help build your list and/or learn more about your business offerings. A bit more is discussed in the section on Advertising.

4. **Website Search Engine Optimization (SEO)**

    Another method to help you get more activity to your website is the process of **Search Engine Optimization** (SEO) which helps maximize the number of visitors to a particular website by ensuring that the site appears high on the list of results returned by a search engine. SEO is an ever changing situation as the search engines change their algorithms from time to time. If you are going to get involved with SEO it's best you work with a person that specializes in this area and get a understanding of the what is being done with your website and to get internet metrics to see a "before and after" of traffic flow to your web site after the SEO optimization has been completed.

5. **Social Media and Blogging**

    Social Media websites and applications that enable users to create and share content or to participate in social networking. Blogging is adding new material to or regularly update a blog. And a Blog is a discussion or informational site.

Here are some current examples of social media:

- **Facebook** is a popular free social networking website that allows registered users to create profiles, upload photos and video, send messages and keep in touch with friends, family and colleagues.

- **Twitter** is a free microblogging service that allows registered members to broadcast short posts called tweets. Twitter members can broadcast tweets and follow other users' tweets by using multiple platforms and devices.

- **Google+** (pronounced *Google plus*) is Google's social networking project, designed to replicate the way people interact offline more closely than is the case in other social networking services. The project's slogan is "Real-life sharing rethought for the web."

- **Wikipedia** is a free, open content online encyclopedia created through the collaborative effort of a community of users known as Wikipedians. Anyone registered on the site can create an article for publication; registration is not required to edit articles.

- **LinkedIn** is a social networking site designed specifically for the business community. The goal of the site is to allow registered members to establish and document networks of people they know and trust professionally.

- **Reddit** is a social news website and forum where stories are socially curated and promoted by site members. The site is composed of hundreds of sub-communities, known as "subreddits." Each subreddit has a specific topic such as technology, politics or music. Reddit site members, also known as, "redditors", submit content which is then voted upon by other members.

- **Pinterest** is a social curation website for sharing and categorizing images found online. Pinterest requires brief descriptions, but the main focus of the site is visual. Clicking on an image will take you to the original source, so, for example, if you click on a picture of a pair of shoes, you might be taken to a site where you can purchase them.

  Social Media and Blogging are excellent methods to get in front of and communicate with your Target Market on a regular basis. You can also find out about current treads and happenings.

6. Video Marketing

Video marketing is incorporating videos into your marketing campaigns, whether to promote your company, product or service. Customer testimonials along with live event videos are becoming more and more popular as companies try to leverage rich media content into their marketing efforts. The website **YouTube** is a free tool to post your videos and link them back to your website. You can also have links in your email marketing going to YouTube videos.

7. Regular Mail – Postcards, Brochures, Newsletters, Letters, "Drip Marketing"

Postcards, Brochures, Newsletters, Letters, are still a very good marketing tool. The world still gets hardcopy media to their homes and businesses. It is highly unlikely this will end any time soon. The challenge with this type of marketing is the "words that are written on the paper". This is called Copywriting. This is another skill that can be learned, however, it may make sense from a productivity point of view to work with a professional is you do not have the time or desire to write copy for your materials.

Drip Marketing is a low cost means of running a marketing campaign. As the concept infers you place a "Drip" (one piece of marketing) in front of a prospective customer. An example of a Drip Marketing campaign would be: sending to a prospective customer list – a Postcard, then a week later a Brochure, then a week after that a Letter and then a week after that following up with a phone call to see if they receive the information and to close with a possible appointment to sell your products/services.

8. Telemarketing

Telemarketing the marketing of goods or services by means of telephone calls, typically unsolicited, to potential customers. This is a low cost tool to reach potential customers in an effective manner. The big **HOWEVER** is that you must know how to do telemarketing (which involves writing targeted sales telephone scripts) and does your Target Market want to get contacted in this manner? If your Target Market does not want to get contacted in this manner, then Telemarketing

would not be a good tool to use for your marketing efforts. There are industries that use Telemarketing as their primary means of marketing. The main industry that comes to mind is Executive Recruiting where most, if not all of the business is transacted by telephone.

9. **Advertising – Newspaper, Magazines, Radio, Television, Internet**

   Advertising is another medium to market to prospective customers. Be it in Newspaper, Magazines, Radio, Television and the Internet. A few words about advertising; you have the same issue as mail in that you must know how to write good ad copy. Another point is you must be into advertising for a period of time. Rarely does a one-time advertisement produce many leads (but it does happen, usually if you are well known name). Finally, advertising tends to be expensive. This is a big factor, especially if you are just starting your business. You don't want to spend $10 in advertising to make $2 in profit.

10. **Trade Shows and Events**

    Trade Shows and Events are an excellent vehicle to get in front of your Target Market. Especially local events like a town chamber of commerce. The advantage of Trade Shows is that they are targeted to specific industries and/or market segments. The bigger trade shows tend to be on the expensive side to host a table but when you are first starting out what you need is exposure to your target market for as little money as possible. Search the Sunday newspapers Business section for a Calendar of Events in your area to see what's going on relative to your Target Market. If you live near a larger city get their Sunday newspapers as well. Many counties now have a local magazine as well. It's a good practice to go to your local library and see what periodicals are available in your area both hard copy and digital formats.

11. Networking – Face-to-Face, On Line

Networking is still one of the best methods to market your products/services be it face-to-face or on line. The thing about Networking that many people do not understand is that it is a process and like any other process, there is a right way and a wrong way to do it. Furthermore, you need to be networking in front of your Target Market. If you sell flowers, it's best you don't network with people that sell car parts and then wonder why you are not successful. Networking will be discussed in a later chapter with the process on how to do it effectively.

12. Public Speaking Engagements

Public Speaking Engagements are another low cost method to get in front on your Target Market. You don't need to be a professional public speaker to do this, but it does help to get some public speaking training. **The worldwide leader is Toast Masters International (www.Toastmasters.org).** All sorts of people go there, from house wives/husbands to CEOs of companies as many people have a fear of public speaking (I attended for several years while in corporate work). The trade shows and events marketing methods, previously mentioned, all need speakers. Especially targeted speakers relative to their market segment.

13. Media Presence – Magazine Articles, Radio, Television

Media Presence is another low cost method to get in front of your Target Market. Magazines, Radio and Television need content or else they have nothing to offer but advertising to their audiences. Magazines usually want a 700-word article on a specific subject for their readers. Radio and television are usually discussion-based formats so they would want questions from YOU to ask YOU in the interview as they know very little if anything about your expertise. Once again, there is plenty of free material on Google and books on the subject on how to get published in magazines and appear on radio and television. I did it and you can do it too!

14. Free Report Give Always

To help you build your internet list, one method as you drive internet traffic to your website is to give prospective customers a "Free Report". This does not have to be long dissertation on the meaning of life just a short primer on your area of expertise. Example, if you're a florist – "7 Things You Need to Know When Buying Roses," if you run a bakery – "How Can Gluten Free Baking Help You Feel Better," if you run a car garage "What You Need to Do Every Winter to Prolong the Life of Your Car". It's a "Win-Win" situation, you build your list and the prospective customers get information they did not previously have.

15. Telephone and Internet Seminars (Tele-Seminars and Webinars)

Using the telephone and/or the internet with Tele-Seminars and Webinars is another low cost method of marketing your products/services. As you build your list you can do email marketing to have prospective customers virtually attend your Tele-Seminars and Webinars where you pitch your products/services.

As mentioned previously, this book is designed to give you "the basics" so your next step would be to learn about the specific topic to the level of detail you require by reading books and learning from professionals in the respect area. The above have been discussed in brief, the most common of marketing methods and techniques. With new technologies, come new marketing methods, so it is a good practice to keep abreast of new marketing methods and practices. Start with Google and enter the topic you are interested in learning about and you will get a host of free and not free resources on how you can learn a lot more on the subject.

Baby Boomer Business Success System® Tip: When using Google, if the subject has more than one word place it in "quotes" (Example: "List Building") this tells Google to find these two words together to give more precise information and not the usual 1,000,000 or more hits. ☺

5c. Target Market(s) and Target Marketing – What is it and Why is it so Important to Your $uccess?

A **Target Market** is a particular group of consumers at which a product or service is aimed. Why is that so important? The short answer is you cannot be everything to everyone. Also, being an entrepreneur, you are limited as to your marketing resources. Say you made a cola type product, and type product was even better than the top three cola manufacturers, could you really compete against them? You may get some marketing traction in a given geography (Which is fine. There are plenty of smaller companies that are successful in their areas that we rarely hear about). But competing with the big players is an entirely different game. **Once you identify your Target then you can market to them, hence the concept Target Marketing.** First, you need to identify your Target Market with as much specificity as possible. Is your Target Market male or female or both, what are their age ranges, where located, ethnicity, social-economic background, race, etc.? Marketing to Baby Boomers is different than marketing to Teenagers or Generation-X. This task may seem daunting at first, however I assure you, as you make sales and you observe carefully who is buying your products/services you start seeing a pattern in your buyers. Once you establish your Target Market (or Target Markets, you may have different Target Markets based on the product/services you offer. Start with one target Market first and become successful at it before looking for other Target Markets) then you can use the various marketing techniques I previously spoke about. Will use myself as an example. For this book my Target Market is Baby Boomers, men and women (sex) born in the United States (geography) born between 1946 and 1964 (age range), all ethnic backgrounds (ethnicity), all races (race). I can go further but you get the idea. Next how do I get in front of this Target Market at little or no cost (remember I want to spend $2 in marketing efforts to make $10 in profits)? Here are a few examples of what can be done: I can summarize this book and submit the article for consideration to Baby Boomer magazines like AARP (American Association of Retired Persons) for publication (free I might add as they need content for their readers). I can offer a ꜱ ecial Report on my website (which by the way helps me build my marketing ⅃ᵔ be used for email marketing). I can get public speaking engagements (which heℎ build my credibility as an expert in the field) discussing becoming a Baby Boomer entrepreneur. Just a brief list of my marketing methods to get in front of my Target Market.

Think about all the junk mail you receive. Why do you keep certain mail pieces to read later and other junk mail pieces you immediately discard? We have all been targeted by vendors that know what products/services we like and how we like to buy them so we keep the mail pieces to read later (and the vendors want us to buy) at our leisure and throw out the ones that our not targeted to us.

5d. Market Research – Boring and Exciting and Why You Need to Do It

Market Research the action or activity of gathering information about consumers' needs and preferences. The more you know and understand your Target Market the better you will be able to determine which marketing strategies to use and what products/services you need to create for that market. You can do market research yourself, it does not have to be elaborate or fancy. It can be as simple as asking a few questions related to your Target Market. It's even easier if you already have customers, then it's just a **Customer Survey.** If you are new at this and don't have customers, then give prospective customers in your Target Market an incentive to answer your questions. An incentive can be a; small gift, a discount on their first purchase, a gift card, etc. You can even use a customer survey company like **Survey Monkey** (yes it's their name - www.SurveyMonkey.com) to do the customer survey for you. You give them the questions and Target Market and they find the people and give you the results. If you don't want to do any of this, then you can pay a Market Research company to do it all for you and give you the results.

5e. Business Value Proposition – The Elevator Pitch!

The Business Value Proposition is an important part of your business and networking introduction. Its purpose is to provide an overview of your business, the benefits and value you have to offer, and to start a dialogue. It should be no longer than 60 – 90 seconds (the average attention span of an adult) in length and should answer the questions: who are you, what you do, what are the benefits of your product and/or service and what are you looking for in a clear, concise manner. The **Business Value Proposition** is also known as: The Elevator Pitch, The Marketing Pitch, The Pitch, Unique Selling Proposition and a host of other names. The **Business Value Proposition** is the vocabulary of business. The business world wants to know what you can do for them in a short and to the point statement.

The Business Value Proposition states: Your Name and Title, What You Do, Who You're Doing It For (Target Market) and the Business Benefits (what's in it for them) in a clear concise statement. You will be using your Business Value Proposition in many different business settings; for example, when business networking, on your website and brochures. It will also be useful when crafting your business Mission Statement.

Let's break it down here and put it all together a bit later:

1. Your Name and Title: People want to know who you are and who are they speaking to. If you are a Solopreneur (one-person company and sub-set of Entrepreneur) it's best to say Owner. While you can say President or CEO, people will expect you have employees, office space, etc.
Example: Hello, my name is Oreste D'Aversa. I'm the owner of Metropolitan Small Business Consulting

2. What You Do? What products and/or services do you sell? Just a one-line summary here. When the person listening gives you more time then you can get into the depth, breadth and scope of the products/services you offer.
Example: I provide business consulting, coaching and training services...

3. Who Are You Doing It For (What Business Population?) The specific business segment you work with. This is known as your "Target Market". The more specific your target market the more interested they will be in your Business Value Proposition.
Example: ... for small businesses, entrepreneurs and Baby Boomers
4. The Business Benefits (what's in it for them): it's nice that you do what you do, but business people want to know the business benefits; how your product or

service can reduce costs, save or make money, increase productivity or do things quicker, faster or smarter. They tell the prospective customer how their business needs will be met. Benefits are always directed to the customer. **Benefits fill either business needs or human needs and motivate purchases. Human needs, for example, such as in the area of fashion where a fashion may not save someone money, but makes them feel better when wearing the item.**

Example: … to help them close deals, increase business productivity and profitability.

Let me put all together here:

Hello, my name is Oreste D'Aversa. I'm the owner of Metropolitan Small Business Consulting. I provide business consulting, coaching and training services for small businesses, entrepreneurs and Baby Boomers to help them close deals, increase business productivity and profitability.

You know you did the Business Value Proposition correctly when the person you are speaking with says: "Tell me more". That tells you hit the target with your message! ☺

It's also a good practice, when appropriate, when using the Business Value Proposition to end with a question to engage the listener so they speak as well. Example of questions: Is this something that you are interested in learning more? Are you the right person to be speaking to about this? Can you recommend someone they can use my products/services? Etc.

Business Value Proposition Exercise

The following exercise is to be written out, critiqued and practiced until it becomes a part of your business introduction and networking process.

Build Your Business Proposition Here:

1. Your Name and Title:

_____

_____

2. What You Do:

_____

_____

3. Who Are you Doing It For (Target Market):

_____

_____

4. The Business Benefits (what's in it for them):

_____

_____

5. Question: Asking a question is a way to promote a dialogue between you and the listener.

_____

_____

Put It All Together Here

_____

_____

_____

_____

_____

_____

_____

_____

_____

_____

_____

_____

_____

_____

_____

_____

_____

_____

NOTES

5f. What is a Marketing Offer?

Your **Marketing Offer** is a tool demonstrating to prospective customers how your product(s) and/or service(s) can help them by showing them that the way they are currently doing things needs improvement, or that your product or service can do something quicker, faster more efficiently, reduce costs, or increase their productivity.

The **Marketing Offer** itself can be a questionnaire or some type of analysis showing areas that need improvement and how your product or service can be used to make that improvement.

For this exercise I will be discussing how to compile a questionnaire type **Marketing Offer**. First, I will discuss the **Components of the Market Offer**

The Components of the Market Offer

Section One – Contact Information

This section contains the basic contact information of the person with whom you are speaking. It will help you in some marketing analyses as to where you are getting your leads or any type of information you would like to capture. Keep things brief as your prospect might become impatient.

My personal **Marketing Offer** is called, **"Entrepreneur/Small Business Success Assessment".**

Contact Information

Date: _____ Lead Source: _____ Industry: _____

Business Name: _____

Primary Contact Name: _____ Title: _____

Address: _____

City: _____ State: _____ Zip: _____

Phone: _____ FAX: _____

EMail: _____ Web Address: _____

Notice the field **Lead Source** (where did the lead come from) so I can match this to my marketing efforts. If I see I'm getting my business from one source, I will invest more energy in that source and cut down my efforts in another. Example, if I am getting most of my leads from public speaking engagements and none from advertising. I will look to book more speaking engagements and stop spending money on advertisements. Also, notice the field **Industry,** I also monitor the industry the prospective customer is in. If I notice a significant amount of interest from one specific industry, say technology, I'm going to work my marketing efforts in that industry.

Section Two – Company Background

Collect some background information about your prospective customer in the **Company (or Person) Background Section**. It will help you better understand your prospect and give you some insight as to the way they conduct business

Company Background

1. How long have you been in business? _____

2. Describe your business and what you sell. _____

_____

3. How many employees do you have? _____

4. How many sales people do you have? _____

5. Have you ever used a consultant or trainer before? _____

You want to ask questions that are relative to the products/services you sell. Example: **Have you ever used a consultant or trainer before?** This tells me if they have worked with outside vendors to help them with their business. If the answer is **Yes**, then I know they understand the value of working with an outside professional to help them with their business so I don't have to explain that to them. If the answer is **No**, then I know that I have to use different sales tactics when talking with them. For example, one tactic would be I would want to educate them on the value of working with someone who has been there and done that so they can save time, money and increase productivity, so they don't have to re-invent the wheel.

Section Three - Business Background

Find out about their business practices or how they are doing things now in the **Business Background Section. If you are dealing with an individual, how are they doing things now in relation to your offering?** Chances are they are not doing anything or are doing things incorrectly or they would not being help in your area of expertise.

Business Background

6. Who is your Target Market? (Industry, Company Size) _____

7. Who is your Target Client/Prospect? (CEO, CIO, VP, GM) _____

8. Where are your Prospects located? _____

9. How do you prospect for customers? _____

10. Are your sales consistent? _____

11. Do you have and what is your Marketing Offer? _____

12. What is working for you in the area of getting clients? _____

_____

11. Do you have a structure for your Presentations? _____

12. How do you prepare for your sales appointments? _____

_____

13. Do you know what your Closing Ratio is? _____

14. Do you know what your Cost Per Lead is? _____

15. How accurately are you able to forecast your Sales Revenues? _____

I ask questions of things the prospective customer should be doing. Then if they are not doing them at the end of the assessment I tell them issues (problems) I found. **What's important here is I don't solve their business problems I tell them what areas they need help, and in reality, they would have to hire me to get the solutions.** Basically, I hold up a mirror up to the prospective customer and show them the problems they have. People don't want to be told to stop smoking, they already know that. People want to come to their own conclusion they need to stop smoking. That's the purpose of these questions to show people their problems and you have the solutions.

Section Four – Problem Analysis

Find out what types of problems they have in your area of expertise in the **Problem Analysis** Section. This area is where you discover their 3 main **"Problems"** from their prospective and how you can solve their problems with your products or services. Let the prospective customer **tell you from their prospective** what their problems as you may have missed it with you questions. Sometimes the problem is easier than you think and sometimes is more complex. For example, I run into situations where the problems are not with the business but they have family members working in the business and they think their business life is an extension of their family life and they run the business the same way. That's the real problem.

Problem Analysis

16. What are your 3 greatest challenges selling right now?

1. _____

2. _____

3. _____

Section Five – Sales Qualifying

Sales Qualifying Section will determine if your prospect is serious about making a change that will lead to buying your product or service. If the answers to these questions are **no** it is highly unlikely you will be selling your goods or services to them. **This section is the bridge between Marketing and Selling in your business.**

Sales Qualifying

17. Are you willing to make changes to your business (or the way you do things)? _____

18. Are you willing to invest at least 4 hours per week in developing your business? ___

19. Are you willing to make the financial invest in your business? _____

20. Do you have any Questions? _____

Discuss the benefits of your services and offer different levels of service.

If a prospective customer is **NOT** Willing to Make changes (Question 17.) and/or **NOT** willing to put the time in for business coaching (Question 18.) and/or **NOT** willing to make the financial investment (Question 19.) they are telling you they are just shopping. **It is highly unlikely that this type of prospective customer will become a customer.** Then just put them on your list (for email marketing) and maybe they will buy at a later time. **This process is called "Qualifying the Prospect" or "Qualifying" and it's the first thing you do in the sales process which will be discussed in sales chapter.**

Let's put my Marketing Offer all together here:

Entrepreneur/Small Business $uccess Assessment

Contact Information

Date: _____Lead Source: _____   Industry: _____

Business Name: _____

Primary Contact Name: _____   Title: _____

Address: _____

City: _____   State: _____ Zip: _____

Phone: _____   FAX: _____

eMail: _____ Web Address: _____

Company Background

1. How long have you been in business? _____

2. Describe your business and what you sell. _____

_____

3. How many employees do you have? _____

4. How many sales people do you have? _____

5. Have you ever user a consultant or trainer before? _____

Business Background

6. Who is your Target Market? (Industry, Company Size) _____

7. Who is your Target Client/Prospect? (CEO, CIO, VP, GM) _____

8. Where are your Prospects located? _____

9. How do you prospect for customers? _____

10. Are your sales consistent? _____

11. Do you have and what is your Marketing Offer? _____

12. What is working for you in the area of getting clients? _____

_____

11. Do you have a structure for your Presentations? _____

12. How do you prepare for your sales appointments? _____

_____

13. Do you know what your Closing Ratio is? _____

14. Do you know what your Cost Per Lead is? _____

15. How accurately are you able to forecast your Sales Revenues? _____

Problem Analysis

16. What are your 3 greatest challenges selling right now?

1. _____

2. _____

3. _____

Sales Qualifying

17. Are you willing to make changes to your business (or the way you do things)? _____

18. Are you willing to invest at least 4 hours per week in developing your business? ___

19. Are you willing to make the financial invest in your business? _____

20. Do you have any Questions? _____

Discuss the benefits of your services and offer different levels of service.

This Marketing Offer concept should take you no more than 20 – 30 minutes to complete. It may even make sense to do it on the phone first so you can maximize your productivity. **Notice how this is now a business process. The first thing you do when you meet a Prospective Customer (face-to-face or if appropriate on the phone) is your Marketing Offer.**

Baby Boomer Business Success System® Tip: The more you are able to make business procedures into business processes the more productive you will be and less of your time will be wasted. You will be working smart as you are already working hard.☺

5g. Your Marketing Offer

Now build your own Marketing Offer. While the example given is geared to a business that offers services products can get used as well. You just have to be more creative with your questions when using products but it's not impossible. You can modify this template to your respective needs. This template is meant just to get you started.

My Business Marketing Offer

Contact Information

Date: _____ Lead Source: _____ Industry: _____

Business Name: _____

Primary Contact Name: _____ Title: _____

Address: _____

City: _____ State: _____ Zip: _____

Phone: _____ FAX: _____

Email: _____ Web Address: _____

Company (or Person) Background

1. _____

2. _____

3. _____

4. _____

5. _____

6. _____

Business (or Problem) Background

1. _____

2. _____

3. _____

4. _____

5. _____

6. _____

Problem Analysis

What are your 3 greatest challenges at selling right now?

1. _____

2. _____

3. _____

Sales Qualifying

Are you willing to make changes to your business (or the way you do things)? _____

Are you willing to invest at least 4 hours per week in developing your business? ___

Are you willing to make the financial invest in your business? _____

Do you have any Questions? _____

Discuss the benefits of your services and offer different levels of service.

5h. The Strategic Marketing Plan – The Money Making Blueprint to Achieve Your Dreams!

The **Strategic Marketing Plan,** a subset of the Business Plan, consists of specific details such as who, what, when, where and how you will be marketing and selling your products and/or services.   Marketing and Selling are two different aspects of your business. Though they are "interdependent" upon one another, they need to be understood and planned for accordingly. The Strategic Marketing Plan is your blueprint on how to reach your business goals. When you are first starting out your marketing goals should be based on marketing activities once your business is "up to speed" (generating revenues) then your marketing goals will be based on achieving sales revenue goals.

Strategic Marketing Plans come in many shapes and sizes. The one below is a simple one designed for you to get going and have successes as soon as possible. It is not tied to the Sample Business Plans in chapter on planning.

On the next pages is a sample **Strategic Marketing Plan** and an exercise to write your own.

NOTES

Sample Strategic Marketing Plan

Your Master Marketing and Sales Plan

Your strategic marketing and sales plan, also known as your marketing and sales plan, is a road map for how you are going to market and sell in the market place. The strategic marketing and sales plan discussed here is a simple one, but it will help you organize your thoughts as to what you are going to do and how you are going to do it.

There is no "one way" to write a strategic marketing and sales plan and there are many books on the subject. This Strategic Marketing and Sales Plan will help you get started immediately to organize your thoughts and be productive as soon as possible.

First, we will discuss the components of the strategic marketing and sales plan. Then you will see an outline of a marketing and sales plan and a sample marketing and sales plan. In addition, you have some worksheets where you can write your own marketing and sales plan.

When writing your marketing and sales plan remember to keep things simple and easy. It only needs to be a few pages as you can always go back and adjust things later. This is a "living document" and you will change things as you see what works and doesn't work.

Components of this Strategic Marketing Plan

1. Objective – What is the purpose of this document (tells the reader it is a Strategic Marketing Plan for a business)? What do you want to accomplish with your business (does not matter if is professional or personal or both)? These questions are to give you focus. Your answers do not have to be long, just make them clear, concise and to the point. This part is also important if you give the Strategic Marketing Plan to a bank or family member for funding for your business. Whoever reads it knows immediately what your plan is and how you are going to execute your marketing goals

2. Mission Statement - In order to write your mission statement, you need to be able to answer the following: Why should this business exist? Who will its customers be and how will it benefit them? Why will they be better off after purchasing your product or service? For examples, go to the internet and Google businesses like your own. It does not matter that the businesses are in other states you want to get an understanding of sample mission statements. Look at large corporations and as well as small businesses. The mission statement boils your business down to the essence of its purpose. Your Business Value Proposition can be helpful with writing your Mission Statement; look at that as well. When writing a mission statement, less is more.

3. Target Market(s) – To whom specifically do you want to sell your products and/or services? The more precise the target the more business sales revenues you will generate. Based on the previous discussion on Target Market and Market Research what population to you want to market your products and/or services. Start off with one Target Market, get some success, then you can add multiple Target Markets (not a requirement).

Start making money first, then decide if you want to grow your business from there by adding more Target Markets.

4. Strategies (Summary Level Strategies): – What marketing strategies will you be using to your target market? How will you be marketing your products/services? Will it be advertising, personal networking, direct mail, internet marketing or any of the marketing strategies mentioned previously? Your market research will determine how to make contact with your target market. If your target market reads magazine(s), then you need to find out which magazine(s) they read and get some marketing exposure in them. If your target market attends chamber of commerce meetings, you want to make sure you go to chamber of commerce meetings and so on. Start with no more than three Marketing Strategies and measure your success from there. Then three more if you are not getting the results you desire.

5. Marketing Activities (Details of Strategies): – What type of activities are you going to pursue to get your name out in the marketplace (e.g. Networking, Trade Shows, Advertising, etc.)? Once you have defined your Marketing Strategies in step four you need to get further details. For example, if you say you are going to use Personal Networking as a marketing Strategy with whom are you going to network? Will use my example of promoting this book. The first thing I do is identify all the Baby Boomer groups in my area. One way is to use a website call Meet Up (www.MeetUp.com). Meet Up is a website devoted to various groups, you can even create your own. Which in this situation, I might just create my own group (I would call it Baby Boomer Entrepreneurs). Remember marketing is also people coming to you. Another example of using another marketing activity would be magazines. I would try to get my article in Baby Boomer magazines (which by the way is free, as their readers need content) or I may choose to purchase some advertising. You get the idea.

6. Goals (Proposed Activity Goals): – What are your weekly, monthly and quarterly goals in the areas of making appointments, closing deals, etc.? Once I have identified the Marketing Strategies and how I am going to implement (Marketing Activities) them, then I'll need to set realistic activity goals about actually doing them. **When first starting out, focus on activity goals, then work your way to sales revenue goals. For example, take an activity goal based on the above.** I am going to attend one (1) personal networking event a week and meet six (6) people. Now let's do the math. That's 6 people times 4 weeks in a month times 3 months in a quarter that 72 people. And that's only using one Marketing Strategy! Another example, I am going to send one (1) article submission a week to all the Baby Boomer Magazines until I have contacted them all both hard copy and virtual magazines (some magazines now are only coming out online only). Let's do the math again. That's a minimum of four (4) magazines a month with the potential of getting thousands of dollars of free magazine media exposure! You get the picture. Start with activities and document them in this section.

7. Territory (Geography): – What is the geographic span of your business? Is it local towns, the state, the region, the country, or the world? Realistically, what geography can you market your products and services to? Though the world sounds exciting to say but the reality is a far different and if you do not have a car that limits your geographic area. While in many large cities, you may not need a car to get around, the real deal is you can't spend 2 or more hours using public transportation lugging around your goods and presentation materials to get to a sales call and do it all again to get back to your office or home. If you are selling your products and services virtually (on the internet) then that's a different story. Here, I will use myself once again as an example. I currently live in northern New Jersey (20 miles from Times Square) and have a car, so a 50 miles' radius from my home is reasonable (that is millions of people in my case and thousands of prospective customers). As well as marketing my products and services online nationally (if people from other countries contact me, that's great, but I will not be marketing to them because I know I can't be everything to everybody).

8. Administration (Business Details): – How will you be tracking and maintaining all aspects of your business? There is a lot information contained in this Strategic Market Plan to manage and maintain. **I assure you the details of all these will be too much for you to deal with.** You **will** be meeting a lot people; call me next week, call me in 2 weeks, you call they are not in and you leave a voicemail and remind yourself to call back, etc., etc., etc. You need some type of automated system to store all this information. You need some type of Contact Management System or Customer Relationship Management (CRM) system. There are many out there to choose from. Find the system you like (based on your needs) and use it. These systems range from the simple to the complex and complicated. In my corporate days I used to use a system called **ACT!** (www.ACT.com).

A very simple Contact and Customer Management System. Now I'm in the process of re-assessing my needs and evaluating different solutions.

End your Strategic Marketing Plan with a date and time stamp:
Last Update: January 20, 2010 5:00pm

Your Strategic Marketing Plan should be reviewed once a year. Keep what works and add new things until **YOU** find **YOUR** system that works for **YOU**. A good time to do your Strategic Marketing Plan is every year between Christmas and New Year's Day. Business is usually slow and it's a good time to observe what worked this past year and plan for the next year. Your Strategic Marketing Plan does not have to be more than a few pages long and once you do the main one the annual updates should go fairly quickly.

Below is an example of a Strategic Marketing Plan. It is the one I started my business to get me to focus on what I had to do to get me started. I kept it simple and to the point, so when I got off track I could refer to it and I know what I had to do to get me where I want to go.

2010 STRATEGIC MARKETING PLAN

Metropolitan Small Business Consulting

1. Objective (s): To create and operate a business to become financially independent, have a comfortable lifestyle and help my family financially.

2. Mission Statement: To help small businesses and entrepreneurs achieve their financial and personal goals by providing business and personal coaching, consulting and training services so more people can live the life they want to live on their terms.

3. Target Market (s): The Target Markets for my business are: Solopreneurs (One Person Businesses; Entrepreneurs (One or More person businesses), Small Businesses (Owner with a few employees) and Baby Boomers. Though Medium and Larger businesses can also use my services the process is often lengthy and time consuming to get their business and not worth the return on investment (ROI).

4. Strategies (Summary Level Strategies):

My strategies are to:

1. **Write books and articles** on the subject of small business issues. This strategy makes me the perceived expert in this field (though I do have 20 years of corporate business experience and 15 years of self-employment behind me).

2. I will **put up a website** to drive traffic to same and will place my website on my business cards, brochures, letters, postcards or anything else that has my business name on it. I will **sell my books** on my website.

3. I will take my **written work and send** to small business publications to get "free professional exposure" and add to my credibility.

4. I will look to get **public speaking engagements in front of my Target Markets** to get free publicity and offer my services (business coaching, consulting and training).

5. I will **send press releases to radio and television stations to get interviews** which will give me the ability to add to my credibility and promote my products and services.

6. I will **personally network locally** with small business groups.

7. I will **contact colleges and universities** and if see if they require someone to teach small business courses.

5. Marketing Activities (Details of Strategies):

1. Write book and summarize book in an article (750 words).

2. Build website.

3. Identify small business publications.

4. Identify public speaking engagements at appropriate venues.

5. Identify radio stations that have business shows and/or business show segments.

6. Network with small business network groups.

7. Contact colleges/universities in the metropolitan New York City area for teaching assignments.

6. Goals (Proposed Activity Goals):

1. Write book and summarize book in an article: Six Months

2. Build website: One Month

3. Contact 3 business publications each week: Ongoing until all publications are contacted.

4. Request public speaking engagements at appropriate venues: Ongoing

5. Send three press releases a week to radio and television stations. Ongoing until all appropriate radio and television stations are contacted.

6. Network with one small business network group a week and meet 3 potential customers

7. Contact colleges/universities in the metropolitan New York City area for part-time teaching assignment: Ongoing until teaching position found. Accept or reject the same based on current work load.

Or use the format below depending on the type of activity goals you have when first starting your business.

    Weekly Goals:

    Monthly Goals:

    Quarterly Goals:

7. Territory (Geography):

The geographic territory to operate my business since I have a car and drive is:

1. Northern New Jersey (all the counties),

2. Central New Jersey (all the counties),

3. New York City (all 5 boroughs) and

4. Long Island.

In this order, as the more I travel the more I must charge for my services.

8. Administration (Business Details):

The administration of information is critical to insure the activities mentioned are carried out and monitored properly. I will be timely in all reports, preparation and delivery of all proposals to prospects, clients and other necessary written and verbal requirements. I will learn and use ACT contact management software to manage my time and prospective customers in an efficient and productive manner.

Last updated 12/28/2010 at 5:00pm

Strategic Marketing Plan Outline

1. Objectives(s):

2. Mission Statement:

3. Target Market(s):

4. Strategies (Summary Level Strategies):

5. Marketing Activities (Details of Strategies):

6. Goals (Proposed Activity Goals):

    Weekly Goals:

    Monthly Goals:

    Quarterly Goals:

7. Territory (Geography):

8. Administration (Business Details):

Last Update: January 20, 2010 5:00pm

Now put it all together here:

Strategic Marketing Plan

1. Objectives (s)

_____
_____
_____
_____
_____
_____

2. Mission Statement

_____
_____
_____
_____
_____

3. Target Market(s)

_____
_____
_____
_____
_____

4. Strategies (Summary Level Strategies)

_____

_____

_____

_____

_____

_____

5. Marketing Activities (Details of Strategies)

_____

_____

_____

_____

_____

6. Goals (Proposed Activity Goals)

Weekly Goals

_____

_____

_____

_____

_____

_____

Monthly Goals

_____
_____
_____
_____
_____
_____

Quarterly Goals

_____
_____
_____
_____
_____
_____

7. Territory (Geography)

_____
_____
_____
_____
_____
_____

8. Administration (Business Details)

_____
_____
_____

Exercise:

Pros and Cons of Running My Own Business

Spend some time reading and completing the Business Plan and Strategic Marketing Plan. Then make a list of the "Pros" and "Cons" of starting and running your own business. This exercise is not designed to dissuade you into not starting your own business but rather meant to give you a "reality check" as what it takes to run your own business.

Pros of Running My Own Business	Cons of Running My Own Business

NOTES

Chapter 6: Sales and Selling Techniques: The "Magic Steps" to Close Every Deal!

Selling – the profession and skill everyone likes to hate! ☺ I'm going to let you in on a very big secret – **EVERYTHING STARTS WITH THE SALE - CLOSING THE DEAL!** You could have the best product or deliver the best service in the world, but if you don't sell it to someone nothing happens!

Selling is the way that you help customers to buy products and services from your business. You need to be able to meet the needs of your customers and provide value for money.

Selling is a skill and like most skills it needs to be learned, practiced and mastered. In this book you will learn and can **immediately apply** proven sales skills and sales processes that have been working for sales and non-sales professionals for many, many years. You're probably using some of these skills right now in your personal life and don't even realize it.

6a. Selling Methods and Techniques

Below are several methods and techniques that you can use to sell your products or services. They are all proven methods and should be used to contact your prospective customers. Should you not be familiar with or feel uncomfortable using a given technique this will be a good opportunity to learn and start applying these techniques as soon as possible.

Telemarketing

Though I spoke about telemarketing in the Marketing chapter here you will receive more detailed information about using the telephone as a method to reach your target audience. It is relatively low cost and you can make dozens of calls each day without leaving your office or home. People have been selling over the phone ever since the telephone has been invented. Even though in recent times the practice has come under fire it is still a proven and time-tested selling technique.

When telemarketing, it is very important that you convey your message with as many benefits as you can as clearly, concisely and quickly as possible. Everyone is very busy and there is no time for small talk. Your introduction should have the following information: Greeting, Your Name, Title, Company, What Product and/or Services you sell with a benefit, and End with a Question to Engage the Listener. For example:

"Hi, I'm Oreste D'Aversa the owner of Metropolitan Small Business Consulting. I work with entrepreneurs to substantially grow sales, increase profits and productivity. Are you the personal responsible for growing revenues in your business?"

You will notice it is very similar to your Business Value Proposition and both are meant to have the listener say to you "tell me more about what you do".

NOTES

Telemarketing Worksheet

Greetings Your Name, Title and Company Name: _____

_____

Product or Service with Benefit(s): _____

_____

_____

_____

Question: _____

_____

Put it All Together Here: _____

_____

_____

_____

_____

_____

_____

_____

_____

Some products and services need to be sold "face to face" and the phone is just a means to get appointments. Other products and services can actually be sold over the phone so you should be prepared to close business in that manner. You should always pre-plan by **writing a script** when telemarketing. Your calls will be easier to make and become a routine exercise. Though you are writing and reading from a script you want to sound as natural as possible.

Direct Mail

Direct mail is another proven method to sell your products or services. The advantage of direct mail is that you will be getting your message into the hands of your target audience. The downside is that direct mail can be costly depending upon on what you send (e.g. catalog, brochures, etc.) and it is labor intensive. If you are going to use this method, I do recommend the following measures to make your mailings as successful as possible:

1. **Know Your Target Market** – You want to know as much as possible about your target market and audience in order to customize your mailing to address their specific business needs.

2. **You Need to Write Ad Copy That Sells!** – This part is a bit tricky. What are the right words that are going to make your reader take action and call you? **Writing ad copy is not like regular writing. It needs to get the reader's attention immediately!** You may want to read a book on how to write ad copy or hire a professional to work with you.

3. **Follow Up with a Phone Call** – A few days after you send your mailing follow up with a phone call. This accomplishes three things; **one** you insure your mailing was received, **two** it demonstrates your follow-up skills and **three** it gives you another reason for your name to be in front of your prospect.

E-Mail

E-Mail is an excellent low cost method to get your message in front of your target audience. Start collecting e-mail addresses from meetings you attend and if you have a web site make sure you have a place on your first page where people can leave their email address. As you collect these e-mails send people a bi-monthly newsletter with tips about your product or service. Keep the content more about helping than selling and keep it short, concise and to the point. People will look forward to receiving your e-mails and it is a very good tool to stay in front of your target audience.

E-mail is an extraordinary tool for getting your message out to the marketplace. You need to be aware of the laws governing the use of e-mail.

The Internet

The Internet has forever changed the way business is conducted. You are now in the position to look and feel like a big corporation at a fraction of the cost and you can sell your products or services nationwide, if not worldwide. With the advent of computer technology and the Internet, business is being conducted much faster. With costs falling and ease of use rising, more and more people are embracing this tool to do business.

You will want to create your own web site where you can describe your products and services. Online customers will visit your website, purchase your products and services and thereby make you money while you sleep! More and more people are doing business over the Internet. **Think of it as your online salesperson.** It's easier than you think to implement a web site so don't be intimidated by the Internet or computer technology. Just think of them as tools to make you more money, more productive and more time efficient.

Person-to-Person

Selling Person-to-Person allows all of your senses to come into play. You can see the person's body language and expressions. It is the single largest type of selling that is conducted worldwide. Because of this, much of the balance of this chapter is aimed at this method of selling.

I do want to mention a very important technique to get you to the person-to-person stage of selling and that is Business Networking and how to network effectively.

Effective networking is much more than merely meeting people, exchanging business cards and engaging in social pleasantries. In a business environment, **you need to network with a purpose**, and that purpose is to get as many *qualified* leads as possible. Noticed my use of the word *qualified*. Getting a stack of business cards may make you feel like you've made some progress, but if no one is interested in your products or services; you have just succeeded in wasting your valuable time.

To be effective, you must first employ a properly designed and executed networking introduction (using your Business Value Proposition). Your networking introduction should not be more than 1 to 2 minutes long (the average attention span for an adult), and should contain your name, title, a brief description of your product or service with a benefit statement, and should end with a question that engages the listener. As an example, I will share my own networking introduction:

"Hi, I'm Oreste D'Aversa, owner of Metropolitan Small Business Consulting. I work with entrepreneurs and businesses to increase their sales revenues. And you are? OR Do you know someone who might be interested in my services?"

I recommend you write your networking introduction, practice it with family, friends, or business associates, or just record and play it back to yourself. Once you have mastered your networking introduction, it will become a powerful technique in your prospecting "tool box". Remember, networking is a skill. Master that skill, and your introductions to people will be very productive. Your time is valuable. Make the most of your networking opportunities and your profits will soar!

Similar to the telemarketing technique, when networking you are talking **about the benefit(s) of your business** and learn what the other person does. It also shows you how others can help you get more business, or put you in contact with other people who can help you further network yourself.

You can have multiple networking introductions based on who you are speaking with at the time of your networking. For example, I perform the business coaching. I coach entrepreneurs and small business owners. I also coach business executives of corporations. If I'm going to a networking event with business executives, I will target my networking introduction to them. Though they are not my main "Target Market" I can coach them nonetheless.

Although the methods are very similar, each one is looking to achieve a different outcome.

Networking Introduction

Greeting, Your Name and Title: _____

_____

Product or Service with Benefit(s): _____

_____

_____

_____

Question: _____

Put it All Together Here: _____

_____

_____

_____

_____

_____

_____

_____

_____

_____

_____

Networking Introduction

Greeting, Your Name and Title: _____

_____

Product or Service with Benefit(s): _____

_____

_____

_____

Question: _____

Put it All Together Here: _____

_____

_____

_____

_____

_____

_____

_____

_____

_____

As you understand your marketplace better, you will see which techniques work best. Perhaps it may be a combination of the various techniques discussed here.

Additional business coaching, training and consulting services are available for all of these areas should you require in depth knowledge on the subject.

Boomer Business Success System® Tip: Remember, **Learn, Practice and Master** the various techniques and you will be proficient in no time.☺

NOTES

6b. The "Seven Key Steps" to Close Every Deal

When you start selling your prospective customer your goods and/or services that is called the **"Sales Process"** or **"Sales Cycle"**. Rarely, on products or services of a substantial amount, does one go from "business networking introduction" to "let me cut you a check" thereby closing the deal.

The profession of selling, like most professions, has its own language or jargon which you are learning as we go along. Someone who is getting "ready to get ready" to buy is a **"Suspect"**. They are suspects in that they are not ready to buy, but have some interest in your products/services. Someone who you are currently trying to sell is a **"Prospect"**, a prospective customer. Someone who you have sold is either a **"Customer"** or a **"Client"**. A **Customer** is usually a transactional (For example: selling a cup of coffee, fixing your car, going to a restaurant, etc.) business relationship while a **Client** is usually a long-term business relationship (For example: an accountant, attorney, architect, etc.).

When we talk about the **"Seven Key Steps"** to Close Every Deal we mean the steps in **Your** sales process. You may have a few more or a few less steps, but for the most part the following are representative of the steps of a typical and basic sales cycle. You may not be using these exact words, but chances are you are finding out this information as you are going along. **The more you can make this into a standardized process (procedure), the more success you will have in closing more deals.** You will notice that if you do not get answers to some of these questions, it is highly unlikely you will get the business (Close the Deal). Let us examine a Sample Sales Process:

Sample Sales Process

1. **Meaningful Conversation (Qualifying)** - You identify what the prospect is looking to purchase, timeframe to purchase and budget (money) available. Begin to establish a connection towards building a business relationship with this person. This is called "Qualifying the Prospect". Do they have the necessary criteria to purchase your products/services?

    If the person you are speaking with **does not** know what they want to buy, **does not** have a time frame as to when to buy it, **has not money budgeted** for this product or service, then **you are not going to close the deal with them** in the immediate short term and you should move on to your next prospect. In selling, always be polite and professional. Simply have the person come back when they have answers to your questions. And the right answers are: **They know WHAT they want to buy, WHEN they want to buy it and have MONEY to buy it.**

2. **Presentation** – A presentation is where to talk about your company, products and services and the benefits you can deliver to your prospect.
    It is very important that you deliver a clear, concise and brief presentation talking about what you can do for your prospect. You will learn more about this topic later in the section called **Presentations**.

3. **Demonstration** – A demonstration is where you actually show your product or service in action.

    Deals can be lost here so be careful. Only show what you know works and only what the prospect is interested in seeing. If it's a service you sell, then give a small sampling of what you do and how you do it.

4. **Identifying Purchasing Process** – Is there more than one decision maker? How do they buy or make their purchases? Do they go home and discuss it with the family? Are other peoples' approval required to close the deal (For example, you are selling interior decorating services and you are speaking to one spouse, but the decision is made by both spouses you need to identify that and be speaking to both spouses or you will not close the deal.)? What are the actual steps for your prospect to make a purchase? How long does that take?

5. **Identifying Financing** – Though similar to **Identifying Purchasing Process here you are finding how the funds (monies) are actually gotten for the purchase.** How does this person buy? Will they be paying with Cash, Credit card or Check?

    You need to find these things out or your deal will stall and not close. If you do not know how their procurement process works, you will not get their business.

6.　**Contract/Agreement Phase** – Once you give them a contract (I prefer the word agreement – sounds less intimidating) how long will it take them to return it to you? Who needs to review it? Who needs to sign it?

It is not a closed deal until you get that contract signed and in your hands. Be persistent; put a self-addressed envelope with your contract (agreement) or offer to pick it up. Do whatever it takes. *You have <u>nothing</u> until you have that signed contract in your hand.*

7.　**Signed Contract/Agreement and Payment** – Congratulations! You've closed the deal! Now process your paperwork, deposit your payment and deliver the goods and/or services and start all over again with your next prospect!

What is YOUR sales process? Identify it step by step, and you won't be wasting time with people who are not buyers. You will be more focused and be closing more business. **It's YOUR business and YOU are in charge, if YOU do not manage YOUR prospects YOUR prospects will manage you!** The Sales Process is a very important sales tool to keep deals moving so you know where things stand to close your deals.

Sales Process Outline

1. **Meaningful Conversation (Qualifying)**

2. **Presentation**

3. **Demonstration**

4.   **Identifying Purchasing Process**

5. **Identifying Financing**

6. **Contract/Agreement Phase**

7. **Signed Contract/Agreement and Payment**

Now identify your sales cycle in the next page.

Your Sales Process

1.   Meaningful Conversation (Qualifying)

_____

_____

_____

_____

2.   Presentation

_____

_____

_____

_____

3.   Demonstration

_____

_____

_____

_____

4. **Identifying Purchasing Process**

_____

_____

_____

_____

5. **Identifying Financing**

_____

_____

_____

_____

6. **Contract/Agreement Phase**

_____

_____

_____

_____

7. **Signed Contract/Agreement and Payment**

_____

_____

The deals you are working on in the various stages of the sales process are called your **"Sales Pipeline"**. Your Sales Pipeline is a very good indicator of your future sales and revenue generation. **The more precise you can get your "Sales Forecasts" the more "bankable" revenues you will be able to deposit.** This also helps your business in the following ways: if you know you are going to make X Dollars this month, you can negotiate better deals with your vendors because you are able to buy more raw materials because you know what deals are coming in. You are able to expand your business; you may be able to hire more people all because you are able to forecast your sales, with some degree of accuracy, what monies are coming in on a consistent basis. Sales Pipelines are used by all many businesses to forecast their Monthly, Quarterly and Annual sales revenues. This is very important, especially if the company answers to Wall Street and the company has investors. Additional business coaching and consulting is available, should you like to implement Sales Forecasting as a business practice.

6c. Preparation Before Sales Calls

Preparing yourself before any sales call, presentation and/or demonstration is critical to your success. It speaks volumes about your professionalism. It prevents you from any sudden surprises in your meetings. Your actions in this, the "Preparation Phase," with your prospect will speak louder than your words ever can.

When in the preparation phase, and for that matter the entire sales process, the sale should be all **about the prospect.** What do they need, want and desire from your product or service? Get a piece of paper and make three columns:

Column 1 – Required (must have),

Column 2 – Would Like to Have (would be nice if you did) and

Column 3 – Wish List (wished you did).

Once you find these things out (from the Prospective Customer), you put them into your presentation. Listen to your prospect; they will lead you to what they want so that you can give it to them. If you sell apples and they want apples, give them apples. Do not try to give them oranges. It will not work and if it does work it will only last for a short period of time and you will lose in the long run.

Ask questions that will lead you and your prospect down the road to buying your goods or services. When do you think you will be making a decision to purchase our window treatments? How will our lawn service be of help to you? In your role as a sales person, you need to let your prospect talk as you actively listen. You should be taking notes as you are actively listening. They will tell you what they want so that you can give it to them. When asking questions, listen carefully to the answers. Those answers will be the key to closing that prospect.

Preparation is the sign of a true sales professional. You will always look good being prepared before any type of sales call. It demonstrates that you care about the customer's potential business and that means you care about the customer. When you care about the customer he or she in return will buy from you. People buy from people. **People buy from people they know, like and trust.** Preparation will close you more business. Being unprepared will lose you more business. It's just that simple.

6d. Presentation Skills

Presentation skills are an integral part of the sales process. It is a skill that you must, at minimum, be comfortable performing and at best must master. There are two parts of presentation skills that will be discussed. Both are of equal importance - public speaking and the components of a presentation.

First, to deliver a good presentation you must be comfortable speaking in front of people. If you have a background in public speaking that's great. If not, I suggest you join **Toastmasters International** (www.ToastMasters.org). Toastmasters is the best way to improve your communication skills. Lose your fear of public speaking and learn skills that will help you be more successful in whatever path you have chosen in life. You can find a local chapter on their web site or your local white pages. It is a low pressure, very professional organization and the dues are very reasonable. You will put to use what they teach you as soon as you learn it and what you learn you will be using the rest of your life.

The second part of delivering a good presentation is the actual components of the presentation. "Presentation Speak" is different than the way one speaks in a normal conversation. Presentations tend to be bulleted items in slides that are meant to be further elaborated upon by the speaker. In the world of presentations, "less is more and more is less".

Now let's get into designing a presentation and the basic parts or components. Most presentations are prepared using a software program called Microsoft PowerPoint. While it is not absolutely necessary to purchase a computer and software, it will make your life easier and you will be able to deliver your presentation on a computer, email it to a prospect, and so on.

Next, your presentation should not exceed 20 to 25 slides and not go past 20 minutes in length. If you go too long in either number of slides or length you tend to lose your audience's attention. **You need to be clear, concise and to the point.** That can all be accomplished in 20 or so slides and in about 20 to 25 minutes. That's why it is so important to be prepared and to have asked questions related to your prospects before delivering your presentation, so your presentation becomes a focused delivery of information to your prospect.

These are six basic questions that you need to answer in your presentation. Your preparation, by asking questions of your prospect to identify their needs, will be of great help in answering these questions.

1. **What is the purpose of this presentation?** – What are you presenting and why?
2. **Who are you?** – What is your professional background and expertise?
3. **Why should I buy from you?** – Why should I do business with you and who are some of your clients?
4. **What do you do?** - What products or services do you sell?
5. **What can you do for me?** – How can you save me time, money, make me money, reduce my costs, increase my productivity or increase the quality of my life?

6. **What are the next steps?** – You want to discuss what is the next step in the process, in order to do business with you.

You will find that by giving each of the six questions a slide or two and some other questions with a few extra slides, you will be able to meet your 20 or so slide limit with no problem. The contents of each slide will contain bullets with one to three sentences each and are really meant to be a reminder to you on the topic so you can further discuss it in more detail. There should be no more than 3 to 5 bullets per slide with no more than 1 to 3 sentences per bullet. An example of a slide is below.

Company Background

- Extensive Sales and Marketing Experience

- Proven Training and Coaching Skills

- Small Business Ownership

In an actual presentation setting, the presenter would go into more detail on each bulleted item and with other slides, answering the other six questions; and be "painting a picture" for the prospect as to the expertise of your company, what you can do for them and why they should be doing business with you.

Additional coaching/consulting is available on "How to Deliver Presentations and Demonstrations that Close More Deals in Less Time".

NOTES

6e. Handling Objections

Believe it or not objections are a good thing and are a normal part of the selling process! It shows that your prospect is interested in purchasing your goods or services.

To be prepared to handle any objection, begin by making a list of everyone you have ever heard. Given the unique characteristics of your product or service, outline how you can use that objection as a selling opportunity. Your list will probably include some of the most common objections; You're too expensive, You have no experience, How can I trust You if I don't know You? Etc.

Handling objections is the most delicate time of the sale, demanding grace and skill. Many salespeople proceed quickly and rush this part of the sale rather than slowing the process down and moving with care.

Instead of listening carefully and attentively, many salespeople are busy forming their rebuttal. The prospect senses this anxiousness and impatience, and in response, becomes more defensive.

Below are some tips to deal with objections:

1. Hear them out:

Don't assume that just because you have heard every objection under the sun that you need not listen fully to your prospect's objection. Your prospect may have a unique twist.

You must completely focus on the prospect to determine the real significance of this objection. Prospects are wary of salespeople who only pretend to listen, and are angered by salespeople who interrupt their objections to refute them.

These behaviors are disrespectful and demonstrate weakness. Be confident and show your concern for their objections.

2. Consider Your Options:

As you are listening, you can begin to consider your initial strategy to minimize, ignore or handle the objection. There are times, especially when hearing "knee-jerk" objections that you will want to ignore the objections and keep on selling.

There are times when you will know that you cannot overcome the objection, but can minimize its importance in the overall picture.

3. Restate the Objection:

By restating or paraphrasing the objection, you show your concern for the prospect and get clarification in case you misunderstood his point. **It also buys you useful thinking time.** Some prospects even withdraw their objections once they hear them spoken aloud.

Paraphrasing the objection can provide you with a platform from which you can better respond to the objection.

For instance, if a prospect says, "Your prices are too high," you may respond by saying, "If I understand you correctly, you are concerned about receiving sufficient value on your investment?" Now, instead of dealing with the issue of price, you can sell the value and benefits of your product or service.

4. Question the Objection:

If appropriate, ask the prospect to elaborate on his point.

You not only gain some valuable time, but during the discussion you may hear the answer to your problem. You will often find that the prospect did not understand a specific point, or that you did not communicate it properly.

If you do not clear this up, the prospect will hold onto his objection and you will lose the sale.

5. Answer the Objection:

Many salespeople skip steps one through four and immediately answer the objection. However, by completing the first four steps, you gain an understanding of your prospect's point of view -- and also earn his/her trust -- enabling you to choose the most meaningful information for this prospect.

Because you have been willing to listen to him, he is more likely to now listen to you.

6. Confirm the Answer:

Once you have handled his objection, check in with the prospect to make sure your response satisfies his concern. "That clarifies the point, doesn't it?" or "With that question solved, we can go ahead, don't you agree?"

If the client says yes, you can lead to a close. If the prospect doesn't feel that his objection has been dispelled, you have some choices.

You can explore the objection further, you can see what else is on his mind, or if there are other unstated objections in the way.

7. Sell Benefits and Lead into the Close:
Once the objections have been handled, review the major benefits for this prospect, and go for the close. Now that you have uncovered the prospect's needs, presented the value of your product or service, demonstrated how your show can meet those needs and set to rest any objections or concerns, then closing the sale is the natural outcome of all that has come before. Ask for the order simply and directly.

You must know your product or service's strengths and limitations and be prepared to handle any possible objection. With the confidence that comes with being prepared, you will welcome objections as your greatest opportunity to sell.

There are many different techniques in handling objections. Find the methods that are right for you.

Uncovering and overcoming objections challenges you intellectually and emotionally. It requires that you know not only your product and/or service, but yourself and your prospect as well. Handling objections successfully can and will increase your success as a salesperson.

6f. Closing the Sale

Empathy is an intimate understanding of the feelings, thoughts, and motives of another. That's why empathy is of prime importance in selling. Empathy is putting you yourself into the prospect's shoes. It's knowing and feeling what your prospect is feeling. It is in knowing exactly how to proceed depending on the information the prospect has given you.

Until you develop empathy for your customers, until you develop the skill of calling for and getting a favorable agreement that sales people call closing, you probably will not make it in selling. The prospect should sense that you understand and care about helping them solve their problems, not that you are just looking for a sale.

As a salesperson, you must truly believe that you can satisfy the prospect's needs. You must see the benefits, features, and limitations of your product or service from your prospect's view; you must weigh things on the prospect's scale of values, not your own; and you must realize what is important to the prospect. Your prospect must always be the star of the show.

Focusing on your prospect enables you to answer the crucial question in any selling situation: When should you close the sale?

Watch for Signs that a Deal is Near

There is a certain electricity in the air when the prospect is ready to go ahead, but here are some positive buying signs to watch for:

- **The prospects have been moving along at a smooth pace, and suddenly they slow the pace way down.** They're making their final analysis or rationalizing the decision.
- **They speed up the pace.** They're excited to move ahead.
- **Suddenly, they start asking lots of questions.** Like anyone else, they ask questions only about things that interest them.
- **They ask questions about general terms of purchase before they settle on one particular model.** Some people immediately start asking questions about the initial investment, delivery, and so on. They feel safe doing this because they know you can't sell them everything. If they ask these questions after you know exactly what they want, it is a positive sign.

Go for a "test close" after you get positive sign. If you think that your prospect is ready to close the sale, try a test question to make sure you are reading the sign correctly. As you get more experience in selling, you will become more proficient at reading body language and other buying signals.

Do Not Short-Change the Process

Some people start relying so much on positive readings that they short cut other vital steps such as qualifying or demonstration. When you short-change the overall selling process, it's hard to go back and restore the steps you skipped. Invariably, shortcutting steps can cause you to lose many sales. Although it is important to become better at knowing when to close the sale, each prospect should get your full attention to make sure you don't come up short at the end.

When you ask a question from which you expect an answer, confirming that the prospect wants to go ahead with the purchase, you want one of two things to happen:

- The prospect gives you a **yes** or an answer that indirectly confirms their desire to go ahead with the sale.
- The prospect gives you an objection or asks for more information to enable them to make a decision.

If you start talking before the prospect answers, you lose control of the negotiations and you gain nothing. You have neither a confirmation to go ahead nor an objection; you wasted your attempt to close the sale.

Would you like delivery on the 15th or the 30th? They pause to think when would be the best time to have the product delivered. You get uncomfortable with the silence and think; *they must be thinking they don't want it.* Then you panic and say, *Okay, how about if I give you another 5% off;* when the total investment wasn't what the prospect was considering in the first place. That's why you always wait for them to respond before you speak, after asking your closing question, and why it is so important to keep quiet after you ask your final closing question. If you have a big mouth, this would be the time to put your foot in it — literally — to keep yourself quiet.

If you start looking around or fidgeting, you distract the customer and let them know how uncomfortable you are. Neither of these scenarios helps you move toward a successful close. Try to focus your stress in a way that they will not see or recognize it as a nervous action.

Closing a sale -- getting your prospect to say yes -- can sometimes be as easy as asking for it. Once you have laid the foundation by qualifying your prospect, discovering their needs, and showing how your product or service meets those needs, it's time to ask for the order. **You can you use the following closing technique:** "Mr./Ms. Prospect it sounds like I was able to successfully answer all of your concerns (objections) regarding our product/service so the next step would be to get a signature on our agreement (contract) OR a deposit, etc.

6g. Using Contact Management Software to Increase Productivity

What is Contact Management Software?

Contact management software is a convenient way of storing information on your "target audience" – i.e. your customers, prospects/leads, suspects, suppliers etc. on a computer. There are many different contact management software packages available on the market; all are capable of different levels of managing information. Most contact management software all have a common feature in that they are built around a database to hold information on this audience.

Why Use Contact Manager Software?

Contact manager is important in today's market place - no matter what industry you are in. As part of your overall marketing strategy, you need to communicate with your market efficiently. It is no good holding data on paper, or across many different databases, email in-boxes or - inside people's heads. You need to hold it all centrally, store information on each company and prospect and have coordinated communications across your business - sharing information.

Contact management software allows you to:
- Increase productivity and better utilize your time.
- Utilize a system to keep in touch with clients, prospects and other important contacts.
- Quickly find contact information on clients and prospects.
- Write letters, emails and send faxes easily.
- Stay focused by automating daily to-dos and schedules.

- View others' calendars and task lists from your workstation.

- Delegate work to administrative personnel.

- Become a "paperless office" with your scanner and scanning software.

Effective contact management is an absolute necessity for any business in today's highly competitive environment. Contact management software gives you a method to organize and manage your contacts that can make the difference in your business.

Additional training and consulting services are available for this area should you require in depth knowledge on the subject.

6h. Conclusion

You have learned quite a bit of information about selling. You are equipped with the proper sales techniques to find, present and close more business. Perform these sales processes regularly and perfect your own sales systems and processes and watch your sales grow!

There are no great secrets in selling, just basic proven methods and techniques, which you are now equipped to perform yourself. **Selling is a skill and like any skill you first need to <u>learn it</u>, then <u>practice it</u> and in short order you will <u>master it</u>.** Use these proven sales tools and watch your sales skyrocket!

NOTES

Chapter 7: Delivering Your Products and/or Services and Making Money: Packaging is Everything for Profitability

7a. Products and Services

It is a good practice, when first starting your business, to create both products and services, if at all possible. One advantage of doing so is it will provide you with "multiple revenue streams" (more than one way of making money). When offering services, it also gives people a chance to work with you, which many times leads to purchasing more products and services from you. For example, if you make earrings (jewelry) it may be a good idea to learn how to pierce ears. I'll use myself as another example. I am selling this book as a product and I also provide services (coaching, consulting and training) in conjunction with the book. The book becomes the foundation of multiple sources of revenue.

7b. Identifying Products and Services

Your first exercise is to identify the Products and Services you are going to sell. When doing this, start with three (3) levels of Products and Services (See below). This is important and will be discussed a bit later.

Level One – Basic Products

Level Two – Intermediate Products

Level Three – High End Products.

Another good practice is to make sure you have more than one vendor for the sources of your materials to create your products, just in case the vendors raise their prices higher than average, cannot deliver on time, go out of business or whatever may happen (truth is stranger than fiction here – one vendor could not deliver because of a union labor strike and the outcome was products could not be made which did not make customers happy).

7c. Pricing Your Products and Services

When first starting your business the following is a good pricing model to start with:

Level One – Basic Products should be priced to make little profit

Level Two – Intermediate Products should be priced to make more profit than Level One Products and lower than Level Three

Level Three – High End Products should be priced to make the most profit.

For example, you make jewelry:

- **Level One – Basic Product** is a pair of custom jewelry earrings, your cost $1.00 you sell them for $5.00.

- **Level Two – Intermediate Product** is a pair of jewelry earrings using commercial metals, your cost $5.00 you sell them for $20.00.

- **Level Three – High End Product** is a pair of jewelry earrings using precious metals your cost $50.00 you sell them for $250.00.

What happens many times is that you sell a lot of Level One and Level Two products on a consistent basis (which we call "bill paying money" because these products pay your bills consistently☺). While initially **Level Three** may not sell much, but you are making more profit when you do sell them. This pricing model is a starting point should be adjusted as needed. For example, if you start your business and customers just want **Level Three – High End Products** then you focus on creating High End Products and/or you hire some to sell Level One and Level Two products while you focus on Level Three – High End Products and really make serious profits. Level One and Level Two products pay your bills and Level Three – High End Products is your "life changing" type profits.

Here's a real life example, take a restaurant for instance. The owner is not getting rich by selling individual entrées (a hamburger plate, a steak dinner, pasta dish, etc.) sure that pays the bills, but the real profits are in catering events where profits are being made in doing volume. A restaurant may cater a 100-person event at $25 a head that's $2,500 per order. Do that once (or more) a week with 52 weeks in a year that $130,000 just in catering not to mention the profits from the restaurant. Though getting an order of that size may not come every week the addition of catering to that business gives the owner the Level Three Products to make higher profits. Here's another idea for the owner of the restaurant; add Level Three Services like event planner, servers and bartenders and make even more profits!

Let's do another example, this time I will use the services. Besides being a Small Business Coach I am a Career Coach as well. The two fields are similar just the terminology is different. In business you use a Brochure to market your business and in a job search you use a Resume to Market yourself. Same concept different tools. Anyway, let me show you the Three Level Model here:

- **Level One Services – Resume Writing** Here I offer a basic resume service. I have written hundreds and have viewed thousands of resumes. As the saying goes; "I can do this in my sleep". I don't make a lot of profit here, however, it's consistent when I do market that service.

- **Level Two Services – Resume Writing and Job Search Coaching** Here I offer resume writing and job search coaching. Make more profit than just Resume Writing with the addition of job search coaching.

- **Level Three Services – Career Services** Here I offer resume writing, job search coaching and career planning for a longer period of time. One month, three months, six months and customized services. Here is where the most profit is made.

7d. Packaging Your Products and Services

Be creative with the above model. **The easier you make it to buy, the more people will buy from you.** Very few people say they like the food at fast food restaurants, what they do like is the conveyance of quick "In and Out" service and the choices they have. Have $10 in your pocket you can get a combo meal (entre, side and a drink). Only have a few dollars in your pocket then you have the "Value Menu" (one item). There is something for everyone in a quick and efficient manner.

In the marketing world, it's said that fast food restaurants are really in the business of convenience and "Big Box" stores are really in the business of saving consumer's money. It's a different way of looking at things, however it's the truth nevertheless.

Another method to "piggy back" with Packaging Your Products and Services is to offer the packages with a Coupon. For example; Use this coupon and get a discount when you buy this package. You see this concept used in retailing. Buy a set of pots and get a coupon for a Dutch oven or get a coupon for a discount towards the purchase.

Get creative with your Packaging Your Products and Services just always make sure you are making a profit. Make sure you "know your numbers", that means you know your costs (materials, overhead, your time, etc.) and you are not giving away your profits.

Packaging Your Products and Services is also another good way to sell off inventory that is not moving. Make a package, give customers a good deal and get rid of inventory that's not moving. **Sure, you make less profit but inventory that doesn't moves makes no profit.** A "half a loaf" is better than none.

The **Level One-Two-Three System** is a good place to start with the Packaging Your Products and Services. As your business grows you can make a decision to keep or grow this system or make a system of your own. For example, you may "hit it big" from the beginning and customers just want your Level Three Products and Services. Then you can shed your Level One and Level Two offerings and just focus on your Level Three offerings. There are many possibilities, do what makes sense. Do what brings in the most profits. Do what makes you happy! That's the whole idea of the Boomer Business Success System. ☺

Boomer Business Success System ® Tip: Packaging Your Products and Services makes it "easy to buy" from you. People don't want to think about all the combinations on how to buy your products and services. You can always customize a package if you need to. Remember; always make it "Easy to Buy" from your business.

NOTES

NOTES

Chapter 8:   Customer Service: The Secret Sauce to Your $uccess

8a. Customer Service Basics

Customer service is one of the main pillars of your success. Customers like to know you care about them even after the sale. This can be done in various ways; with a phone call (if applicable), an email or by having a mechanism if they need to get in touch with you if there is an issue with your product/service. Many a time I have stayed with a company or **spent even more money** on a product/service because of the quality of their customer service. For example, I use a well-known cellular phone provider, while their fees are higher than their competitors any time I have a problem (nationwide) I get it resolved by either calling their customer service number (24 hours a day) or going to a local store and the problem gets resolved quickly. While like most people, I do not like paying more money for anything, having relatively little or no down time on my mobile phone is more important than paying a few extra dollars a month for cellular service. People will pay for high quality customer service for they know if there is ever an issue, it will be handled in a quick, efficient and courteous manner.

Customer service does have a very important purpose in your business and must be delivered in a high quality manner. Besides being a necessary function in your business, it can be what makes or breaks future deals with current customers and prospective future customers. With the creation of the internet more and more people go to the internet to check reviews before making a buying decision. I, for example, shop on a large internet website (sounds like a jungle ☺) and before I make a purchase read the reviews on the item. Many a time (I would say 50% of the time) I **DO NOT** purchase an item because of bad reviews. Reviews like; the product breaks quickly, customer service stinks, there are no replacement parts, etc. Conversely, when I see very good reviews I feel good about making that purchase. The products I really am comfortable purchasing, is when I see 25 or more buyers and no one posts a negative review. Sure enough, when I get the item it a good product.

As your business grows, you may want to hire employees, and customer service becomes even more important as your employees become a reflection of you. By training good customer skills and employee accountability you can insure consistent quality customer service. Later in this chapter you will see a **Customer Service Form** that I designed (use this one or design your own based on your business needs) to keep your customer service needs answered uniformly when customers call in with an issue. Whoever answers the telephone at your business and there is a customer issue to be dealt with, this form must be filled out. At the end of the week, you review these forms and observe the issues and see what can be improved and incorporated into your business. For example, you make dresses in colors: blue, green and yellow. Customers call you and ask will you be making the dress in red as it is a festive color for the holidays and Valentine's Day. If you see that mentioned enough times on your call sheets it would probably be a good (Strategic Planning) decision to start making red dresses next season. You get the idea, have a formal process to manage, record and analyze customer service calls. It really is an easy way to make more money with your current products/services.

8b. The Business Side of Customer Service

Marketing Surveys

A **marketing survey** is an objective and systematic collection, recording, analysis and interpretation of data collected about existing or potential markets for a product and/or service. The marketing survey will tell you what potential customers and/or current customer want, like and/or don't like about your products/services.

Market surveys can be administered in various ways. Paper surveys or questionnaires that businesses email or hardcopy postal mail to customers are common forms of market surveys. Often you will see businesses such as restaurants and service type business often use questionnaires to gather feedback about their experience with their company. Some businesses conduct market surveys over the phone, while others conduct surveys electronically via email or through third-party websites dedicated to market surveys.

Market surveys help all types of businesses make better business decisions about the types of products and/or services they offer, decisions about pricing, how to handle competitors and whether to enter or get out of the market. Review and analysis of market surveys can prevent a business from making a costly mistake such as launching a new product or service that does not fulfill a need in the market, getting into a market that is saturated with competitors and setting prices too high or too low. Surveys can help entrepreneurs assess the viability of new ideas. You may love your product/service however the market survey is telling you different. **You must have a "non-emotional"**

perspective when reviewing your market survey information as sometimes it may not be what you want to see or hear about your product/service. Remember, you are running a business and looking to generate sales revenues and make profits. **Your ego must take a back seat to your profitability.**

Referrals

Who are the very best new customers you get? Who is most likely to buy from you and continue being a good customer in the future? Isn't it a prospective customer who was referred to you by another customer who is an advocate for your business?

Referrals make for the best prospective customers because they have already developed some trust for you and your company. Their defenses are down and their minds are open. These are the ideal conditions for making them new customers.

The most expensive customers to get are those in the "cold market," through advertising or other marketing activities. Yet that's where most of the marketing effort for companies seems to go. You can market much more effectively by devoting more of your time and resources to developing referrals.

Let us examine how you can encourage your customers to give you more referrals.

1. You must deserve referrals. You have to deliver products and services that people can't stop talking about.

2. You must ask for referrals. At the end of every sales interview, whether you make a sale or not, you should ask for referrals. When you make a sale, you have only completed one-half of your mission. The other half is to get referrals. To encourage the customer to make referrals, help him isolate people in his or her mind: Is there a business associate, like him or her, who you can talk to; a customer; a supplier?

3. Show appreciation. This is the real key to continue receiving leads from a customer and cultivating him or her as a center of influence. Thank the customer for making the referral. Write a thank-you note. Call the customer with a report of the results of your interview. Give thank you gifts in appreciation: send flowers, take him or her out to dinner, or give tickets to a show or athletic event.

Your Customer Base

What is the highest return you can make on a marketing investment? Try encouraging your existing clients to purchase additional products or services that are complementary to what they already buy from you.

In a regular sale, you must pay for the cost to acquire the new customer. However, when you bring in additional sales from your existing customer base, the costs to acquire these sales are as little as one-fifth the price you originally paid to acquire the customer in the first place. So it makes a great deal of economic sense to invest a portion of your marketing budget toward increasing sales to your current customers.

Here are a few low-cost ways to market additional services to your existing client base:

- **Personalized Letters:** You can send personalized letters to your customer base by using any type of inexpensive mail merge programs. Optimum frequency is once a month, but *do not* send too many letters as your customers may grow tired of your message.
- **Email Newsletter:** Offer your customers the opportunity to receive an email newsletter with tips and suggestions as to how they can get more out of their buying experience, while you soft sell additional products or services you can offer them.
- **Invoice Stuffers:** This is normally one-third of a sheet of paper that you stuff in a regular invoice envelope already addressed to a customer. These little promotions of your products or services cost you next to nothing—and no extra

postage is required. For those of you than don't send paper invoices, you can always market your services in the email version of the invoice you send to your clients.

- **Call Them.** This is such an obvious sales tactic, that many of you would never think to call customers just to pitch a new product or service to them. But if you don't call your customers, they may never know how much more you could do for them. I recommend you call your customers once or twice a year to see how they are doing and let them know about some part of your products or services. You should already be calling your business customers at least once every month or two just to show them how much you care about their business.
- **Ask for Referrals:** As mentioned earlier always be asking for referrals.

So don't forget your customer base. It is a goldmine just waiting to be mined!

8c. Processes and Procedures

Below I have created a Customer Service Call Form. As mentioned in previous chapters you want to create processes and procedures in your business wherever possible. This will save you time and times is money. If you are going to be doing the same procedure over and over again, make it easy on yourself. Make a form; it will save you time and energy.

Furthermore, when you hire people (so you can spend time working on large deals, generating sales revenues, running the business, etc.) you can use the processes and procedures and training tools so everyone in your business is "speaking the same language" of your business. So when you say, there a customer service on line two, everyone in the business knows enough to have a **Customer Service Call Form** ready to take the call. And when you say let's discuss the call you just took, an employee is coming to your office with a form so you can see what transpired on the call and how it was handled.

NOTES

Customer Service Call Form

Call Number: _____ Call Worker: _____

Date and Time of Intake: _____ Order Number: _____

Contact Information of Customer:

First Name: _____ Last Name: _____

Business Name: _____

Address: _____

City: _____ State: _____ Zip: _____

Phone: _____ FAX: _____

EMail:_____ Web Address: _____

Product and/or Service Issue:

Product and/or Service in Question? _____

_____

_____

What is the Problem, Issue or Question? _____

_____

_____

_____

_____

What is the Resolution? _____

_____

_____

_____

_____

Called Closed By: _____ **Date and Time:** _____

NOTES

Chapter 9: Conclusion - And the Beat Goes On...

Well, you've done it, you have learned and completed the Boomer Business Success System ®! You have the knowledge on running your own successful small business as well as making a difference in the world while enjoying the lifestyle that you choose.

Let's review the Boomer Business Success System ®.

- In **Chapter 2: What Baby Boomers Need to Know**; we started out giving you the background and data points of being a Baby Boomer. Though statistical in nature, it is important none the less.

- In **Chapter 3: Your Life's Purpose . . . What's it All About Alfie?** You have the tools to examine your life's purpose. We're all here for a reason and a purpose you now have the ability to find yours. And don't be afraid to meditate you'll be a better person for it ☺

- In **Chapter 4: Strategic Business Planning: The Power of Planning Your Work and Working Your Plan** begin by planning your business and working that plan you will have a guide to reach your financial goals.

- In **Chapter 5: Marketing You Go to the Marketplace, Even Better the Marketplace Comes to You!** You learned some basic methods of marketing and the secret weapon of the "Marketing Offer" so people will come to you! I love when the phone brings and people call me about my marketing offer ☺

- In **Chapter 6: Sales and Selling Techniques: The "Magic Steps" to Close Every Deal** you learned that selling does not have to high pressure or uncomfortable thing just ask the right questions and have a "Sales Process" and you'll be closing deals in no time!

- In **Chapter 7: Delivering Your Products and/or Services: Packaging is Everything for Profitability** you learned that by putting your products and/or services in packages (bundles) people will tend to buy more. Let's face it, who doesn't like a deal? Remember, always make it easy to buy!

- In **Chapter 8: Customer Service: The Secret Sauce to Your $uccess** in this chapter you learned that good customer service is not just good business, but there is prosperity in your customer base by; market research – ask what they like about your products and/or services, what other products/services they would like and make and sell them and the power of **Customer Referrals**. Customers have bought from you already so they are likely to buy from you again.

As you can observe from the graphic below the five pillars of business success are in essence parts of a wheel that goes around and around. The **Strategic Business Planning** supplies the **Marketing** which feeds **Selling** that Delivers the **Products/Services** which needs to be tended to by **Customer Service**. These are the keys to running a **$uccessful Business**.

You now have the knowledge to get to where you want to go in your life while becoming financially independent. Add the life experiences and wisdom of your life and there will be no stopping you! Live the life you are truly meant to live. Do your "real work", be of service to others, help make the world a better place and enjoy your life.

Until we meet again, my wish for you is a life of prosperity, good health and love ☺

NOTES

Chapter 10:   Small Business Resources

Web sites and resources for the Small Business Owner:

Amazon.com
Find the book you need from millions in stock.
http://www.amazon.com/exec/obidos/redirect-home/smallbusinessr05

American Express Small Business Network
Ideas, information and money-saving benefits from American Express.
https://www.americanexpress.com/us/small-business/

CCH Business Owner's Toolkit
Cut costs, increase productivity with downloadable checklists, interactive employment tools and more
http://www.toolkit.cch.com

Center for Women's Business Research
Conducts studies and surveys of female entrepreneurs, their management practices, financing sources and more
http://www.cwbr.org

Entreworld
The Kauffman Center for Entrepreneurial Leadership offers articles, tips and more for starting and building a successful business.
http://www.entreworld.org

Entrepreneur.com
Entrepreneur Media offers information, services and advice for small-business owners
http://www.entrepreneur.com

Federal Contracting Made Easy
CPA Scott Stanberry at Management Concepts has written a book that is sure to help anyone who wants to win federal contracts. Who can pass up such opportunities in this economy?
http://www.managementconcepts.com

Harris InfoSource
Profiles of 750,000 companies from manufacturing, technology and service sectors. invaluable for business planning research, sales and marketing and more. Fees apply.
http://www.harrisinfo.com

Home Business Journal
Directory of home business, articles, advice for people running businesses from home
http://www.homebizjour.com

Home Business Magazine
Online edition of publication for home-business entrepreneurs and telecommuters
http://www.homebusinessmag.com

Idea Cafe
Ideas and information about planning, financing, starting and running a small business.
http://www.ideacafe.com

Library Online
Looking for letter templates; prewritten, customizable business letters; valuable tips for writing business letters? This is the place.
http://www.libraryonline.com

My Own Business

A free, online 12-session course that provides the basics for entrepreneurs. This site has plenty of help for both start-ups and already operating ventures
http://www.myownbusiness.org

National Association for the Self-Employed
More than half the businesses in America are run by the self-employed. Get information, insurance and more.
http://www.nase.org

National Association of Women Business Owners
Premier organization for women entrepreneurs with chapters nationwide
http://www.nawbo.org

National Federation of Independent Business
News, views and tools on politics and business management from the small-business advocate with 600,000 members from every industry.
http://www.nfib.com

Out of Your Mind and Into the Marketplace
Write the best business plan for guiding growth and success and for finding capital for your business
http://www.business-plan.com

Publicity Insider
Designed for small businesses and entrepreneurs, PublicityInsider.com contains the latest how-to PR techniques, Internet promotion strategies, editorial opportunities, press release samples and more.
http://www.PublicityInsider.com

QuickBooks Users
QuickBooks is the top accounting software for small businesses. This site offers plenty of help for small business owners, independent bookkeepers, accountants and accounting clerks.
http://www.QuickbooksUsers.com

SCORE
Service Corps of Retired Executives, with chapters nationwide, provides free business counseling in person or online
http://www.score.org.

Small Business Administration
The federal agency that works with small-business owners, providing hundreds of articles on start-up, financing, management and government contracting
http://www.sba.gov

SmallBusiness.com
Articles, advice and recommendations for small-business owners
http://www.smallbusiness.com

Small Business Insurance Center-The Hartford
The site explains the different types of coverage for small businesses, translates dense insurance jargon into plain English and provides tools to help analyze specific coverage needs, minimize risk and even develop a disaster recovery plan.
http://sb.thehartford.com

U.S. Legal Forms
Offers wide variety of legal forms from incorporation documents to bill of sale to contracts.
http://www.uslegalforms.com

Young Entrepreneurs Organization
Global, nonprofit educational organization for entrepreneurs under 40 whose companies have annual revenues of at least $1 million.
http://www.yeo.org

NOTE: Sometimes website links change. If the website address does not come up then

place the name into Google and try it that way as well ☺

NOTES

Notes and Bibliography

Footnotes

Chapter 2:   **What Baby Boomers Need to Know**

[1] Website - http://www.History.com/Topics/Baby-Boomers

[2] Website - http://www.CNN.com/2013/11/06/us/baby-boomer-generation-fast-facts/

[3] Website - http://www.ImmersionActive.com/Resources/50-plus-facts-and-fiction/

[4] Website - http://www.ImmersionActive.com/Resources/whitepapers-and-research/ - PDF File Pre-Retiree Profile

Bibliography

- Boehman, Jonathan and Weigelt, David. **Dot Boom: Marketing to Baby Boomers Through Meaningful Online Engagement.** Great Falls, VA: LINX Corp., 2009.

- Fairley, Stephen, G and Zipp, William. **The Business Coaching Toolkit: Top 10 Strategies for Solving the Toughest Dilemmas Facing Organizations**. Hoboken, NJ: John Wiley & Sons, 2007.

- Hicks, Esther and Hicks, Jerry. **The Law of Attraction: The Basics of the Teachings of Abraham** ™ Carlsbad, CA: Hay House. 2006.

NOTES

www.ingramcontent.com/pod-product-compliance
Lightning Source LLC
Chambersburg PA
CBHW072051020426
42334CB00017B/1466